China & Europe: The Turning Point

CHINA & EUROPE
The Turning Point

DAVID BAVEREZ

Westphalia Press
An Imprint of the Policy Studies Organization
Washington, DC
2022

CHINA & EUROPE: THE TURNING POINT
All Rights Reserved © 2022 by Policy Studies Organization

Westphalia Press
An imprint of Policy Studies Organization
1367 Connecticut Avenue NW
Washington, DC 20036
info@ipsonet.org

ISBN: 978-1-63723-809-7

Cover and interior design by Jeffrey Barnes
jbarnesbook.design

Daniel Gutierrez-Sandoval, Executive Director
PSO and Westphalia Press

Updated material and comments on this edition
can be found at the Westphalia Press website:
www.westphaliapress.org

*For Louis, Arthus and Louis,
imbued with the perfumes of Hong Kong
since they were young,
future builders of "Great Bridges Forward".*

Contents

Foreword xi

Preface xiii

1 | Sunday – Zhongnanhai, Politburo Standing Committee, Speech by Xi Jinping, General Secretary of the Chinese Communist Party 1

2 | Monday – Beijing, at the restaurant called " 1949 The Hidden City", Jean Baguette 5

Election or selection? 6

Reform is not something to be made in small measures 12

Xibercracy or cybercracy? 21

3 | Tuesday – Shanghai, at the Long Museum (West Bund), Professor Leonarda da Vincierra 31

"I shop, therefore I am" 31

"Gucci is an attitude" 42

The Chinese dream of "4.0 Marxism" 48

4 | Wednesday – Emeishan (Sichuan), Lord Fitzbacon 59

The re-Orientation of the 21st century 60

The Sino-American "Cold Peace" 72

Eurasia Felix? 79

5 | Thursday – Shenzhen, on the Huawei campus, Dr von Sprungdurch-Technik 93

An obsession with growth 93

(cont'd.)

Three windows for Europe 103
Putting a stop to the "Yuan-way-street" 108

6 | Friday – Hangzhou, at Alibaba's head office, Magnus Flatpackson 125
Disintegrating the value chain 127
Dematerializing production 137
Disintermediating distribution 148

7 | Sunday – Zhongnanhai, Politburo Standing Committee, Speech by Xi Jinping, General Secretary of the Chinese Communist Party 157

Postface 161

"I would rather be a man of paradoxes than a man of prejudices."

Jean-Jacques Rousseau

Foreword

The view that Europeans have of China is often colored by preconceived – and frequently wrong – ideas. One of the most common errors is to enjoin China to choose sides – is it to be an ally or an adversary of the West? That is not the way to approach the problem. One has to look at China from an objective, rational standpoint. To quote Xi Jinping, China is an economic and political power "with Chinese characteristics". The *raison d'être* of this book is to offer a new vision of the future relationship between China and Europe. It is the author's belief that, in the 21st century, China and Europe should build a bridge between them, in the same way as a bridge was built between the Old Continent and the USA during the last century.

It is not every day that one has the chance to talk to the Chinese president, so this is where fictitious meetings come into play – a cunning way to make such conversations possible. David Baverez has chosen the typically European format of the "political fable" to create a series of conversations between Xi Jinping and five European experts from France, Italy, Germany, the UK and Sweden. Xi receives these guests in places that are emblematic of power, the economy and Chinese technology (Beijing, Shanghai, Shenzhen, Hangzhou, and Emeishan in Sichuan province).

The president converses with each one of his guests, arguing, responding, denying, analyzing and outlining new ways in which there could be cooperation – even alliance – between Europe and China. After engaging in all-encompassing discussions on the history, culture, society, values and aspirations of each, both Chinese and Europeans progress to a mutual understanding of their different visions of the future. It is Xi Jinping who emerges as the one to whom the conversations have come as the biggest surprise. When he gives an account of them to the Standing Committee of the Party's Political Bureau, he admits: "I initially saw Europe as a declining reserve of resources to exploit. [...] I have changed my mind. I think there is more to gain by setting up a "Chinese-style" cooperation between our two ancient civilizations."

Preface

"When my information changes, I change my mind. What do you do?"

John Maynard Keynes

How can I tell them? How can I make them understand? For almost 10 years now, every time I am on a plane traveling back from Hong Kong to Paris, these two questions always haunt me.

The twofold gamble I took when I relocated to Hong Kong in 2012 has paid off: firstly, that the most important effect of the Great Financial Crisis of 2008 would be the return of China to the world stage; secondly, that, despite the magic of the internet, the West would continue to ignore this.

Paradoxically, I have chosen writing – the Old World's preferred means of communication – to tell my friends in the West about the New World of the Chinese "Roaring 2020s", a world built around a society of fervent ambition, whilst our own society is becoming a society of fear.

Just like China, I have no fear of paradoxes. The "anti-China" reader will doubtless find confirmation in this book that I have sold out to the Chinese Communist Party, and yet I have never had any contact with it. However, my views may also provoke the "pro-China" reader to threaten me with a long term of incarceration in Stanley prison in Hong Kong! I welcome both points of view.

When I asked the iconoclastic head of a CAC40 company how he determined the optimum ratio between debt and equity on his balance sheet, he replied: "When my bankers yell at me as loudly as my shareholders!" And yet, one has to try and create a dialogue between European values and Chinese concepts – maintaining the right amount of respect for each of the two cultures – to see if there can be any compatibility, or eventually any future complementarity.

With the way things are at the moment in the world, one cannot really envision such an approach, so why not resort to one's imagination, disciplining oneself to remain serious and yet not taking oneself too seriously? I have therefore chosen to imagine a series of fictitious encounters between President Xi Jinping and a number of European experts – whom he would have chosen for both their skills and their human qualities – to discuss contentious issues with a directness that goes counter to the current political correctness. For the issue for me is to insist on the fact that we should neither love nor hate China, for that would merely reinforce the opinions of people who already have their own fixed ideas. The issue is to analyze a "systemic rival" as objectively as possible, with the aim of attempting to turn it to our advantage in the future, without defending it at the same time.

It is my personal belief that the 21st century should build the same sort of bridge between China and Europe that the USA and Europe managed to build in the 20th century. It will take a century to do it, so it is up to my generation to take the first step and lay the foundations. It will be up to future generations to decide if they want to take their inspiration from Pierre Mendès France when he complimented Jean Monnet on the construction of Europe: "You have succeeded because you didn't know it was impossible."

I hope that, because the characters I have chosen and the topics I have covered are so diverse, the five fictitious dialogues that follow will encourage readers to build their own "Bridge to the Future".

I also hope that, since these encounters are the fruit of my own imagination, readers will be gracious enough to reserve any admonitions they may have for myself alone.

1

SUNDAY – ZHONGNANHAI, POLITBURO STANDING COMMITTEE

Speech by Xi Jinping, General Secretary of the Chinese Communist Party

My dear Comrades,

I have heard that there are some among you who regularly complain that, as a body, you are not involved enough in the decisions that I take. I have therefore taken it upon myself to convene this extraordinary meeting, on a Sunday, in order to outline a pioneer project that I intend to carry out this week. We all know that we are currently at war with the USA, and will be for several decades. We are beginning a new Long March and I have arrived at the conclusion that the factor that will determine the outcome of this conflict will be the position taken by Europe. It is both old and wealthy, therefore particularly vulnerable, and access to its resources, with or without its consent, will play a crucial role. Today, Europe is still rooted in the 20th century and continues to lean towards the USA. We must therefore act without delay, either to tip it in our favor, or to access its know-how before this becomes excessively taxed by Washington.

In order to do this, we must refine our strategy. To this end, I have completely freed up my diary for the coming week. I have set up five private meetings – one every day – with European experts who have been recommended to me both for their diversity, which is a reflection of the rich human landscape of a civilization just as old as ours, and for their forthrightness.

On Monday, I shall be talking with the highly influential Parisian editorialist Jean Baguette about political regimes. My aim is to persuade him that, now that France has once and for all fallen into the Southern European camp, any reform of his country must be steeped in the formulae that have spelled success for us over the last four decades. On Tuesday, I shall be receiving Professor Leonarda Da Vincierra from the University of Perugia who, I am told, is the greatest Italian sociologist of our time. My idea is to see how the Italians can be won over to our side, since Italy is the weakest link in the European chain. Its over-indebtedness has already begun to push it into our arms, and it is the only European country, at this stage, to have joined our "New Silk Road" initiative. Wednesday will be a more difficult prospect: I shall be talking with Lord Fitzbacon, the kingpin of the House of Lords International Relations and Defence Committee. I have to convince him that, after Brexit, it is in his country's interest to join us in building a new world order. On Thursday, the conversation should be easier: I shall be welcoming Doctor von Sprungdurch-Technik, who is the CEO of the German company Von Sprungdurchtechnik GmbH, a world leader in its industrial sector. His company has been so successful in China that I should have little trouble in persuading him into closer economic cooperation. The final interview will be with Magnus Flatpackson, whose name will certainly be familiar to you. He is the youngest partner of the Wallenberg family office in Sweden, based in Stockholm, where he is in charge of investment in the digital revolution. I want to persuade him to look towards the Greater Bay Area rather than towards Silicon Valley.

We shall meet again next Sunday at the same time, when I shall share my conclusions with you. However, I am sure that they will confirm my current analysis: that Europe is an old fortress that can be taken by storm! So you can already start thinking about an action plan to put into effect.

Does anyone have any questions? No? Well then, I wish you all a pleasant Sunday evening with your families. And, next Sunday, make sure you are on top form!

2

Monday – Beijing, at the restaurant called "1949 The Hidden City", Jean Baguette

> *"Freedom has never helped to found any long-lasting political edifice; it crowns the edifice when time has made it solid."*
>
> Napoleon III

– My dear Mr Baguette, I'm delighted to welcome you to this restaurant, called "1949 The Hidden City". This date means a lot to me, as does the Peking Duck which is a specialty of the house and awaits you at the end of our interview. You will see that, behind closed doors, this temple of Chinese gastronomy can also, at times, take its inspiration from the best of French cuisine. This is the spirit that I would like to see as the guiding light of our interview. I'm especially grateful that you have accepted my invitation because I asked to talk about political systems, and I foresee that we shall not be in agreement over a good many points. However, please feel free to say exactly what you think. There may well be some sharp exchanges, but I shall not hold this against you as this conversation is completely private. I know that, in the Elysée Palace, no one is supposed to contradict the President of the Republic when he makes a speech. My aim today is to prove to you that China is always open to dialogue. May I begin by asking you what it is that surprises you most about our system?

– President Xi, I'm sure it will be no surprise to you when I say that for a man to reach the age of 100 is quite something, but when the Communist Party does the same, it's a huge achievement. And, what's more, to be still in power after all that time, well… for a Frenchman and a fervent democrat like myself, it's simply a mystery.

Election or selection?

– So, you want to know the secret of the CCP's longevity… I hope that, by the end of this interview, I will have managed to convince you that the acronym doesn't just stand for the Chinese Communist Party, it stands for Chinese Civilization Party. Our civilization has always been so complex that it seems to be full of contradictions, and a Cartesian culture like your own finds difficult to understand this. If you look back only at the last 40 years – since Deng Xiaoping – you will notice that dealing with our paradoxes has led us to take a new direction every 10 years, sometimes more brutally than the West could have imagined. This is why we never reach the point of collapse; "we fail to fail", confounding the predictions of so many of your brilliant Western forecasters. But you would be right to point out that many of our so-called Communist comrades in other countries have not managed to tread the path of much-needed reform.

"The country that fails to fail"

– What are the greatest paradoxes that you believe we in the West are mistaken about?

– First of all, the relationship between economic and political freedom. Even quite recently, the Western press has highlighted this issue with regard to the status of Hong Kong, but this was already the subject of much heated debate in the West in the late 1980s. The break-up of the Soviet Union proved that uncontrolled political freedom leads to collapse, then to the destruction of economic freedom, and then – with a toxic turn of the circle – to restrictions on political freedom. We, on the other hand, have shown for four decades that strict political control at our stage of development is a pre-condition for economic success. What you see as a paradox is an ever-shifting progression. Ponny Ma, the CEO of the Tencent group, puts it very well: "I sleep with the Communist Party, but we are not married to each other."

– How long do you think these restrictions on political freedom will remain tenable?

– I can't answer that question. All I can say – from a pragmatist's point of view – is that, for many centuries now, 5% of China's population has ruled over the other 95%. In the past it was the mandarins; today it is the 90 million members of the Communist Party. It has done so for over 70 years now and, as your General de Gaulle said when he was almost 70, the CCP is not beginning some "career as a dictator". It is merely the continuation of our historical tradition.

– The genius of De Gaulle was in being a dictator without people realizing it – either at the time or afterwards. I doubt that such subtlety will stand the test of time in your case.

– The main thing is that the CCP will stand the test of time.

– But isn't there the risk that, one day, the 95% will rise up against the 5%?

– The risk is that harmony will be lost. You French people think that a society's harmony is founded on human rights, even when these rights without responsibilities lead some of you to put on yellow vests and smash store windows. Even back in the 19th century, Tocqueville observed that, whereas America had chosen freedom, France had chosen equality. Today, your *gilets jaunes* are demanding both, and if you don't do something about it, in the end, they will have to give up both. In China, we put common interest above individual rights.

– What other paradox should I take into consideration?

– The juxtaposition of state capitalism and what is undoubtedly the most dynamic private entrepreneurship in the world, which never ceases to surprise me. I expect this system must seem paradoxical to you. When it fell to me to appoint a leader to oversee the building of Xiongan, the new "smart city" south of Beijing, I chose a man who had headed up the Pudong Planning Committee in Shanghai in the 1990s and was already retired. He told me, "I'm sorry, but I don't believe in a planned economy." I told him that was precisely the reason why I'd chosen him. So, you see, this is why China will always surprise you!

– But aren't you afraid of contradictions?

– Contradictions are what inspired the English saying, "In order to go right on economics, go left on politics". In politics, you always need right and left in a government. The left, made up of brilliant minds, is proficient in dealing with the macroeconomy, but the realities of the microeconomy just don't get through to them. The right is usually in tune with the microeconomy, but is unable to understand the complexity of the macroeconomy.

– What are the influences that shaped your politics?

– As I've already said, first and foremost, I am heir to an ancient civilization, so my political cocktail is impregnated with Confucian values that place the common interest above all others – values that I would like to combine with my attachment to Mao's views on equality and, more recently, to the reforming skills of Deng Xiaoping. This is what has led me to point the finger at three enemies: shadow finance, extreme poverty and pollution. The first problem was largely dealt with in 2015, the second is in the process of being eradicated, and the third is our priority for the years to come.

The pyramid structure

– In your opinion, what is the best political structure?

– The democratic pyramid structure. At the base of the pyramid, local elections designate those who govern the organization of everyday life. Generally speaking, the West doesn't realize that a large number of local elections take place in China every year. Then, moving up the pyramid, when the issues dealt with have more and more impact on the wider population, the more they have to be discussed by experts, who are the only ones qualified to take the right decisions, even if those decisions are unpopular in the short term. This is the only way of ensuring competency at each level. These days, this appears to be sadly lacking in your so-called democratic model in the West.

– But the Covid-19 crisis seems to have shown up local weaknesses, typified by the Wuhan authorities, and this suggests that your over-centralized system is detached from the realities of the provinces.

– This is where we're going to disagree. Let me surprise you by quoting one of your iconic writers, Albert Camus: "People do not need hope, they need truth." In China, it's the opposite. At our stage of development, the people don't have to know the whole truth about all our problems, but they must retain the hope that we can solve those problems in the future.

– Whenever efficiency is used to justify attempts to obscure the truth, it always ends badly. Why should your case be the exception?

– Because your criticism of provincial authorities has already been taken on board. You will have noticed that heads rolled in Wuhan after the failings pointed out by Doctor Li Wenliang's warnings. What always surprises foreigners coming to China is the high degree of decentralization – each region has highly extensive powers, particularly where finance is concerned.

– But did you have to lie to the whole population about the number of deaths from Covid-19 in Wuhan? Your people all know now that 42,000 nurses were not dispatched to Wuhan from all the other Chinese provinces just to take care of a few thousand patients.

– To the best of my knowledge, the local authorities didn't lie. They produced the Covid-19 fatality statistics "with Chinese characteristics", using the traditional method of linking the cause of each hospital death to the pathology that was stated when they were admitted. In Wuhan, it was very often diabetes, obesity, or respiratory or cardiac failure.

– Well, history alone will judge… There remains the problem of how leaders are selected at each level. In Chongqing, you've deemed it necessary to fire two leaders in succession: Bo Xilai, your enemy, and Sun Zhengcai, who started out as one of your protégés.

Selection, a fool's paradise?

– I can see that the eminent Parisian political scientist that you are is about to pose his favorite question: is it election or selection? My answer to that is all about following the upward slope of the democratic pyramid. You start with elections at the base, then the further you climb the slope of the pyramid towards technical issues, the more you need selection to get people with the necessary skills.

– Aren't you worried that your pyramid will end up like shelves: the higher they are, the less useful they become?

– If selection were based on competition, as in the American Ivy League universities where only individual performance counts at the expense of the common interest, I would have my doubts. Especially if I were to find out that, over the years, these universities had received $6.6 billion of unreported gifts which, oddly enough, seem to have had no effect on admissions! It is not for nothing that, when foreign heads of state visit Xian, we take photos of them surrounded by the vast army of terracotta warriors. It is a reminder to them that, more than anything else, our system of selection will always be based on the common good.

– And yet, Chinese friends of mine have drawn my attention to the fact that the GDP figures for 2018 had to be significantly revised downwards in the provinces around Tianjin. Couldn't it be said that the people in charge of these provinces are the illustration of the old adage, "The official makes statistics and statistics make the official?"

– In a country of 1.4 billion people, you can never get rid of all the black sheeps, and there will always be flaws in the selection process when there is a danger of corruption. But at least we won't end up with a system like yours, in which the only two issues that might unite the nation – the environment and Europe – have seen so many ministers come and go: in 16 years there have been 14 for the first and 11 for the second! Any action in these two areas can only be a credible unifying factor if it is taken over a long period, so you really can't lay claim to that, can you?

– Even so, that system is preferable to the other extreme – lifelong tenure. Isn't that true?

– I've no idea what you are alluding to. In my own case, it was simply decided to allow my term of office to be renewed more than once. You must agree with me that, if the USA had been clever enough to adopt that policy, Barack Obama would still be president. And I think it safe to say that, if that had been the case, the world would be in a better state right now. Why put a talented person out to grass after only eight years?

Reform is not something to be made in small measures

– But, historically, it has only been weak countries that have granted full powers to just one man. Isn't your country much weaker at the moment than you think?

– A country's strength depends on the talent of its leaders. How would you define political talent at this present moment when there is obvious conflict between the old democracies and the rising "*démocratures*" – a term I believe you use for regimes that are a combination of democracy and dictatorship. For me, the answer is in the art of reform, for today, all systems are having to reinvent themselves to face up to the new order. And the problem we are all facing is the paradox of the new pair of shoes: "It is only after wearing them for a while that you will find out if they really fit."

Dragon versus *Drag-on*

– How do you see the question of reforming your country? Den Xiaoping may appear to us to be the man behind "the Transformation of China" – to quote the title of Ezra Vogel's biography, but what about your predecessor, Hu JunTao?

He seemed to have been infected by our president, Jacques Chirac, for after the 2008 financial crisis, he preferred to race down the road of debt rather than instigate much-needed reforms. And then you came along in 2012 with the promising message that market forces were increasingly important. And yet, as from 2015, you have finally given preference to state-owned enterprises. I'm confused. Am I missing something here?

– As usual, your confusion results from an initial misconception. For me, reform has never been something to be understood as a restructuring along liberal lines – which is the only way you see it in the West. Rather, the question has always been to know how to improve the efficiency of our system's bureaucracy, notably by taking a new look at our choices: recentralization as against decentralization. This is the crux of the matter for any Chinese government.

– And how do you intend to go about it?

– First of all, pragmatically – by learning from others' mistakes. We study declining economic models, so as to avoid their own fate. Japan's model in the 1990s teaches us about the danger of an overvalued currency, an asset bubble linked to indebtedness, and the prolonged support of "zombie" businesses. The USSR under Gorbachev shows the absolute priority of economic reform over political reform. From Europe, we learn that the welfare state is to be rejected – it has a cancerous effect on the economy at a time when there is an ageing population. And the USA tells us of the dangers of the illiquidity of a real estate bubble based on sub-primes, and a health system whose costs have become exorbitant because of a cartel of private interests.

– Does that mean you never make mistakes?

– Of course it doesn't! We aren't as arrogant as your American friends! The difference is that we try to correct them as quickly as possible. Take the example of Covid-19 in Wuhan. We made two mistakes. The first was not being able to know the actual state of health of the population at that particular moment; this is something we are now able to do by means of the widespread use of the "medical passport". The second was the initial lack of communication with the local population about the reasons for lockdown and how it would operate, and we're working on this now.

– And that's where you believe the secret of your success lies?

– No, the secret is in clever timing which, by definition, is the opposite of your "at the same time" principle, which may well be very attractive, but disastrous when it comes to execution. Let's go back to the example of Wuhan. We adopted a very aggressive stop-and-go strategy, playing off economic constraints against health constraints – the very opposite of "at the same time". In January, we gave full priority to economic constraints; in February it was health constraints; in March we prioritized re-starting the economy. We took a series of risks, but the result is that less than 10% of the population have been in lockdown, and we have maintained growth in our GDP for 2020. Bear in mind that the true Chinese virus is not the one in Wuhan; it is reform, which guides us every day. It's exactly what your former president, Nicolas Sarkozy, condemns. For him, today's democratic consciousness is preventing projects from coming to fruition rather than helping them to materialize. This is what I call "Dragon versus Drag-on". For instance, we are building a seventh ring-road around Beijing, 1,000 km long, whilst you are still planning to build your Greater Paris. In 1898, remember, it only took a year to build your first Metro line!

"Zerontocracy": zero interest rates, zero reform

– But don't you feel that this unprecedented economic crisis we're going through because of Covid-19 is going to provide a new jump-start for Western democracies?

– I have the impression that it will be quite the opposite. In your country I can see the beginnings of what I call "zerontocracy" – a mixture of gerontocracy and zero interest rates that will only hasten your decline. It's no surprise that your young president's policies are old ones, and are for old people – the ones who elected him!

– It's true that, at the last presidential elections, there were 2.5 times more voters over 65 than under 35. In the USA recently, voters could only choose between four 70-year-olds who, unfortunately, hadn't yet retired: Trump, Biden, Warren and Sanders. The gap between our younger generations and politicians will only increase this trend in the future. Old people, who still favor deflation, are delighted by cancerous zero interest rates that are bound to undermine our economies.

– You are on the way to an acute "Japanization", so shouldn't you take a look at Japan? There you'll see exactly what's going to happen to you over the next 20 years. Even before Covid-19, almost $13,000 billion worth of the world's Treasury bonds already had negative interest rates, including Greece in November 2019 – an economic aberration. And, naturally, since the Covid-19 crisis, the situation has worsened – most of all in Europe.

– But don't you think this is just a passing anomaly?

– I don't think so. For the first time in history, you have a majority of lawyers on the Governing Council of the US Federal Reserve Bank and the European Central Bank.

These men and women are undoubtedly highly qualified in their field, but they are totally ignorant of the economic consequences of the financial decisions they are taking.

– We've come a long way since the highly-respected William M. Martin reigned over the Fed for almost 20 years, from 1951 to 1970. He summed up his mission in a few chosen words that illustrate his free spirit: "Take away the punch bowl just as the party gets going". Such a rigorous attitude is hard to find in the current president of the ECB, Christine Lagarde, who broke the sound barrier of stupidity when she said in March 2020 – right in the middle of the stock exchange crisis linked to Covid-19 – that the ECB was "not here to reduce spreads" in a time of crisis. Only her predecessor Jean-Claude Trichet had shown more incompetence when he raised the European rates in June 2008, a few months before the collapse of Lehmann Brothers!

– Compare that to the people in charge here: Zhu Xiao-Chuan, who headed up our central bank – the PBOC, the People's Bank of China – from 2002 to 2018, was the true savior of the world during the 2008 crisis. He was behind the Chinese 4,000 billion RMB recovery plan that aimed at repairing the ineptitude of Ben Bernanke, the Governor of the Federal Bank, who proclaimed loud and clear that real estate prices in the USA would never fall. Even today, the People's Bank of China is the only major central bank in the world that refuses to monetize the mountain of debts incurred in order to revive the economy. It is this bank that will finally make it possible to end the dollar's status as the world's reserve currency. You have to admit that it would be paradoxical for the US currency to maintain this status when President Trump – who doubled the budget deficit – and the governing council of the Fed – which doubled the size of its balance sheet – have injected an extra $8,000 billion into the US economy in the space of only two months – 40% of the US GNP! Whereas our RMB, which is still non-convertible, is the only major world currency protected by its central bank. Our pyramid structure is far more efficient that your democracies that are being held hostage by their ageing population.

– But won't the swelling public debt eventually force our governments into restructuring themselves?

– Unfortunately for you, the opposite will happen. Look at the Japanese precedent: persisting zero interest rates, together with the inability to ever pay back the principal of public debt, will favor runaway deficits. "Zero interest rates" equals "zero reform of the public sector"! This is particularly true for your country, which is surely the only one in the world where people protest in the streets in their yellow vests to demand… that the world stays as it is!

– As my friend Patrick Boucheron – who teaches at the Collège de France – puts it so well: "The French live in a past that is too glorious for them!"

– I was struck by television pictures of negotiations about pension reform. There wasn't anyone under 50 at the table! If I'd been your government, I would have convened at least as many people under 30 as over 50 – it's the only way to get a truly cross-generational social contract. And young influencers would be threatening to launch an internet campaign calling on the under-30s to boycott future pension contributions!

– But I'm willing to bet that the European social model will surprise you in the years to come because of its faculty for reforming itself.

– I would welcome that piece of news. But how is that going to be made possible?

A pro-active CSR at last

– Through our entrepreneurs who are up against a changing world every single day. If you ever get the chance to meet the Dean of the INSEAD European Business School – Ilian Mihov, a truly brilliant Bulgarian – he will tell you that his wildest dream would be to send an email every Christmas to all those who had graduated over the previous five years, saying: "Your MBA is due to expire on 31st December. If, by that date, you haven't enrolled in a training course, your MBA will self-destruct." It's another way of putting an end to grandfathering, which has now disappeared from the world of international business.

– An interesting approach… Are you sure this Dean doesn't have Chinese ancestors?

– In the future, pressure on us and on you is going to come from the new consumer-citizen. Remember that, at the last European elections, it was the green party that got the highest percentage of votes from the under-35s: 25%. In 2008, three promises were made to our people. First of all, no more debt after the deficit caused by the financial engineering of the first decade of the 21st century. Secondly, more equality, in reaction to the indecent bonuses awarded to bankers. Thirdly, we no longer make irresponsible use of the planet and exploit it, but rather become the guardians of the environment with a care for sustainability. And what is the result? A decade later we have a mountain of extra public debt created in just a few months in the spring of 2020, an unprecedented inequality of wealth distribution, and a global pandemic the extent of which hasn't been seen since 1918! Three promises to the next generation broken threefold.

– I hope you'll note that my country is the only one of the major nations of the world to have drawn up a plan of attack on those same three fronts.

– But what's the point of going it alone when these are problems facing the whole planet? If we in the West also decide to go it alone, we'll soon find out that we have neither the financial means nor the right people. The notorious "State comeback" much vaunted by our ministers is merely an admission of failure. As for the right people, you're the first to go on a desperate search for them among our politicians when you visit the West.

– That's nothing new. Your Aristide Briand was already kind enough to warn us that "Diplomats are only dangerous when they start to work."

– That's why your answers will come from our entrepreneurs, under pressure from their consumer-citizens who will be demanding that every company should not only provide goods or services, but also make a contribution to changing our way of life. For 10 years now, what we have been calling CSR – corporate social responsibility – has only been perceived as reactive: how to pollute the planet as little as possible, how to reduce carbon emissions more and more every year, and so on. The next decade will see the blossoming of a far more stimulating "pro-active CSR".

– What do you mean by a "pro-active CSR"?

– The fact that social and environmental responsibility will be transferred from the public sphere to the private sector. Let's keep France as an example. Its welfare benefits account for 32% of GDP and 58% of public expenditure – a world record, and yet it is still unable to guarantee social harmony. We have to stop dreaming of reform that will have some magical effect, and look at the field of education. How can we combine transmission and innovation? The current problem with teaching is how to know what knowledge to impart to students when the World Bank predicts that 40% of jobs created over the next decade will be in professions that don't exist today. In practice, the vast majority of these jobs will be posted on the online platform LinkedIn, in anticipation of market needs. At the same time, the GAFA – who have been scandalously silent throughout the Covid-19 crisis – will be obliged to pay a monthly universal payment to each of their subscribers, enabling them to finance their professional retraining.

– That has already been suggested by William Ding, the brilliant founder and CEO of the NetEase video game group, during the last CCP Congress: to make all Chinese elementary schools provide classes in coding, which he proposed to sponsor.

– Personally, I don't see how our luxury giants are going to be able to continue surfing on the wave of the explosion of social inequality without contributing to equal opportunities by increasing access to education. This is what a "pro-active CSR" can do: it's no longer a question of vainly trying to defend the negative externalities of your business model to the rating agencies; it's all about helping to rebuild our societies in the digital era, including in areas of activity that are not necessarily directly linked to your own. Let me take another example. In February 2020, before the Covid-19 crisis, the Veolia group, a world leader in environmental treatment, announced it was creating a new air treatment division. It was anticipating a future in which this would become as important as its current operations in water and waste treatment. As privileged Westerners, we have always believed that air was a free natural resource. We shall soon discover that a breath of fresh air, just like a mouthful of spring water, is something that has to be paid for.

– All this makes me think I should meet your entrepreneurs more often than your ministers.

– In any case, you won't have any other choice but to do so; even you as a political leader won't be able to avoid reinventing yourself when you're up against the tidal wave of digitalization that is on its way.

Xibercracy or cybercracy?

– I can assure you, I am perfectly aware of the problem, for it was the first issue I had to deal with when I came to office in 2012. The problem was that the previous team of Hu Jintao and Wen Jiabao hadn't seen the rise of social media coming and, when I arrived, the media were so well established that there was no way I could close them down. It was the example of Hosni Moubarak that finally convinced me on this – after banning Twitter in Egypt, he couldn't hold on to power for any more than three weeks.

WeChat, the world's leading democrat

– So what did you do ?

– Like any good Chinese person, I attempted to turn a threat into an opportunity. I ignored my entourage who advised me to use any means at my disposal to put a brake on the growth of social media. I told myself that they would be a great source of information about the country's social situation. I realized that WeChat is in fact the greatest democrat on earth: it brings together almost a billion people, which means I can feel the pulse of the land I govern. I no longer have to go through the hierarchy of regional and district leaders – who are dangerous intermediaries because they don't always want to tell me the truth. The "direct democracy" that you Westerners are promising your people has already seen the light of day in WeChat. I get a daily report that keeps me up to date with the "top ten" topics discussed by my fellow citizens. I know all about their concerns, their desires, and their frustrations. And it's because I saw my people's increasing concerns about the environment on WeChat that I became convinced of the importance of following their drift. Consequently, I persuaded the CCP to make a U-turn on the issue and, in the end, I signed the COP21 agreement in 2015.

– But, for you, it's also a tremendous surveillance tool, isn't it? Especially with your planned social ranking.

– As always in China, things are are more complicated than that. The social media make it possible to have an approach that is as responsive as it is repressive. In China, if you're simply repressive, you won't last long. I seem to remember that your former president, Jacques Chirac, quoted one of his favorite proverbs to my predecessor Jiang Zemin, whom he had met several times and became close to: "You can't move a donkey when it's shitting." This applies just as much to China as to Mr Chirac's homeland. The whole art of this approach has been in highlighting the responsive side, given our people's expectations. Social ranking has become symbolic: for you, it means losing points because of your innate antisocial behavior and being prevented from taking the train or the plane in the future; for the Chinese, it means the opportunity to join the live streaming or social commerce community, with the prospect of receiving reliable advice on the best products and services to purchase from the overwhelming choice that's on offer. You see it as a restriction on your freedom, whereas the Chinese see it as liberating. That's why WeChat is a wonderful tool – a marvelous sort of Swiss army knife that can enable my people to re-establish a social bond, and enable my government to be more attentive to their needs. Let me remind you that, because I am not elected, I can only claim legitimacy in the eyes of my fellow citizens from the degree of efficiency with which I govern their country.

– You have invented a new model for government – "Xibercracy!"

– I would be grateful if you would explain it honestly to your compatriots in the West. Anyway, in the end, they will have to give it the recognition it deserves, for it is a model that will become more powerful in the critical time we shall shortly be living through.

Tech-cracy rather than tech-no-cracy

– Are you about to give me a scoop?

– I'm simply talking about the second wave of the digital revolution that will arrive during the next decade. This is no scoop for readers of the *China Daily* or the *Global Times*, who mention it every day. But, for a good many of your fellow citizens, it may well come as a big surprise to their everyday lives. What we have to talk about today are the political repercussions of this for you in France. And, of all the Western countries, you are undoubtedly the best able to grasp them.

– Are you suggesting that France should lead the West? Flattery will get you everywhere!

– Flattery usually works when I meet your ministers, but, for once, my remark is sincere. Only the French will understand if I compare my situation to that of Napoleon III, or "Louis-Napoleon the Great", which was the title of the fascinating biography by Philippe Séguin, one of your few recent statesmen. Think about it. Louis-Napoleon was elected first President of the French Republic in 1848 by universal suffrage. He had not long returned from exile in England, whose power was expanding because it had welcomed the Industrial Revolution with open arms. He now had to govern France, which was still mainly rural. With a mandate limited to one four-year term of office, he soon realized that if he wanted to effect the radical transformation that France needed and make a success of it, he needed time. Therefore, in 1851, he organized a *coup d'état* and took care to gain majority approval for it by means of a national plebiscite that gave him full powers. He has gone down in history as the man who modernized France in the 19th century, with the help of highly talented "entrepreneurs" like Baron Haussmann.

– Not everyone admired him though. Victor Hugo also became one of the century's legendary figures for his repeated attacks on Napoleon III.

– Maybe, but of the million Chinese tourists you see in Paris every year, far more visit the Galeries Lafayette – in Haussmann's buildings – than the extremely educational Victor Hugo museum in Place des Vosges.

– But what has this to do with your own situation?

– The technological revolution facing me – that of artificial intelligence –will be of historic dimensions and will naturally have major social implications. For this, I need extended powers over a long period of time, and my comrades now understand this. Since 2008, we have simply been accumulating a huge pile of debts, increasing our indebtedness to almost 100% of our GDP, twice as high as Western countries during the same period. So I also have to deal with being a decade behind, if we don't want to end up like you.

– What philosophy will govern your actions during this crucial period of the next ten years?

– It can be summed up in one word: "tech-cracy" – trusting in the fact that speeding up the adoption of technology will hasten China's development, just as the USA did in the 20th century.

– You can see this already in the difference between political reactions to the Covid-19 crisis in the USA, Europe and China. In the USA, in the space of a few months, a budget deficit of over 15% of GNP and the doubling of the central bank's balance sheet injected almost $8,000 billion into the economy, essentially to benefit the major US groups close to the president: private equity funds like KKR or Blackstone, and industrial groups like Boeing who were lent $60 billion, even though the 737 Max is still grounded! A rather disenchanted American political leader told me recently: "In 2008, we rescued bankers who had $50 million bonuses; in 2020, we rescued private equity partners with $500 million of carried interest." The aim was clear: to maintain the global strike power of the major US groups. In Europe, we chose to prioritize social harmony. France has doled out the tidy sum of €20 billion every month to pay people to stay home, and this artificially maintains the overly-high standard of living of our population.

– While in China we have opted for technologies of the future: almost a third of our investment in the recovery plan– no less than $400 billion – is being devoted to the "new infrastructure".

– And that's all the more surprising since you yourself have no background in engineering, unlike your predecessors who were usually engineering specialists – often in electrical engineering or hydraulics.

– It is precisely because my entourage is made up of people trained in political science, the social sciences or law – including some who have trained in the USA – that we are able to take a rational view of what technology can bring us, and see all of its potential. Compare this to the way the Covid-19 crisis was handled politically in the USA. For me, the American refusal to take account of scientific evidence with regard to public healthcare has marked a turning point in the country's history. Such a spectacular rejection of science – that I call "tech-no-cracy" – will only hasten the decline of the USA in the coming decades. The Washington Post – my apologies for using this source – has estimated that, every day, on average, President Trump lied or made erroneous statements six times in 2017, 16 times in 2018 and 22 times in 2019… yet without diminishing his popularity.

– I'm afraid your comment is not only applicable to the USA, but partly to Europe too: France was incapable of getting the StopCovid app adopted on a large scale during lockdown, even though a fascinating report by France's foreign trade advisors in China – "Covid-19: technology monitor on innovations in China" – listed 92 technological innovations developed in the space of only a few weeks to hasten the end of lockdown in China.

– Technology can be surprising, including in the political arena: in Italy, the *Cinque Stelle* movement achieved its first stupendous electoral victory thanks to an e-campaign that cost the party 9 cents for each vote gained, as opposed to $8.5 spent by the traditional parties.

– It's the end of the line for elections dictated by money! The only way of getting the younger generations interested in direct democracy will be internet voting, like the regular e-voting that takes place in Switzerland.

– To top it all, these young people are not fully aware of the tactics that have been brought in as a result of these technological upheavals. We saw an example of this in 2019 during the Hong Kong student revolt. They had occupied the buildings of the Chinese University of Hong Kong, but what they didn't expect was that all teaching went online the next day. The building they were "holding hostage" didn't only lose any value whatsoever as a negotiating tool, their occupation of it meant that they were delivered into the hands of the Hong Kong police who had surrounded it!

– I can certainly agree with your thinking on this, but I remain convinced that there is one even more determining factor in politics that will come into play in the years to come.

– And what's that?

" Jacinda Mania"

– Leadership! It's going to make a massive comeback and will make all the difference. We've already seen it during the Covid-19 crisis – and it won't have escaped you that the countries that have coped best with the pandemic are headed up by women.

– And what do you put that down to?

– Well, it's partly due to the circumstances themselves. Forgive me for risking a generalization here, but, when it comes to healthcare problems, women see the urgency and gravity of a problem better than men. Apart from that, it was a time when both decisiveness and humanity were called for and no one evinced this combination better than the New Zealand Prime Minister, Jacinda Ardern. She managed a *tour de force* that you could never achieve!

– Are you saying that New Zealand, that little country with its five million inhabitants, should be a model for the world? I sincerely doubt it. What has this woman done that is so exceptional?

– When she was due to speak to the nation on television, she arrived five minutes late, dressed in sweatpants and said apologetically, sitting on the couch in her living-room: "The baby wouldn't go to sleep." She then went on to announce drastic lockdown measures. It was a subtle mixture of extreme empathy and extreme resolution, and it triggered a real "Jacinda Mania" worldwide. You will never get this in the USA, where, traditionally, all elections are played out as a fight between the two symbolic values of each camp: virility on the one side and empathy on the other.

– So are you advising me to have another baby? I'll mention it to my wife, but I very much doubt I could convince her. Don't you have any advice that is a little more practical, so that we can bring our interview to a close on a positive note?

– I would suggest you think about the Notre-Dame cathedral in Paris. For two reasons: for me to make a request and to present you with a challenge. The cathedral was badly damaged recently by fire and its spire collapsed – not part of the original building, but added on in the 19th century by the architect Viollet-le-Duc who took advantage of the occasion to incorporate a representation of his own face, probably so that he could survey the building from on high for ever more. The cathedral is being restored and when it came to choosing a new spire, President Macron decided not to use a contemporary architect to design a different spire. Instead, he chose the *status quo* – an identical replica that would be a reminder of the timelessness of the building. This was an "act of state" in total contrast to the disruptive architectural choices of past presidents – President Pompidou for the Beaubourg Center and President Mitterrand for the Louvre pyramid – both of which have received universal acclaim.

– I think we share the same reading matter. I remember seeing your president on the cover of a recent issue of *Time* magazine, under the title "The Next Leader Of Europe – If Only He Can Lead France". Not everyone can play God…

– This brings me to my request. Come and inject our European leaders with Deng Xiaoping's three bywords: "Vision, determination and courage", because they seem to be missing all three of them. So much for my request. Now, the challenge. Donations have come in from all over the world to help fund the rebuilding of Notre-Dame, and yet, in 2001, the plight of the World Trade Center only received donations from Americans. Notre-Dame's case proves – if proof were needed – that it belongs not to France but to all of humanity. If the Temple of Heaven burned down today, I would bet that donations towards its reconstruction would only come from China. Your challenge is this: as the sun goes down on your "Mandate from Heaven", make it so that donations would come from all over the world.

– Now that's a challenge I like! Unfortunately, I now have to leave you but, as a sign of my gratitude, please allow me to arrange a private visit of the Temple of Heaven for you, before you leave Beijing. You will have the echo wall all to yourself, and you'll notice that, in China, it's not a wall of lamentations! And don't forget the guide! I've already promised him he'll get a good tip if you become the first foreign benefactor… Until then, enjoy your Peking duck!

3

Tuesday – Shanghai, at the Long Museum (West Bund), Professor Leonarda da Vincierra

"What do you think of Western civilization?"
"I think it would be a great idea!"

Gandhi

– Professor, I am delighted to make your acquaintance. Thank you so much for accepting my invitation to come and talk with me here at Shanghai's Long Museum in West Bund, founded by my friends Liu Yiqian and Wang Wei. After our interview, I have arranged for you to have a private visit. I'm sure you will appreciate the collection of Chinese art, ranging from traditional and revolutionary through to contemporary. As my advisers have explained to you, I would like to strengthen mutual understanding between the Chinese and European civilizations and I would like our conversation to be as free as possible. So, may I leave it up to you to ask the first question?

"I shop, therefore I am"

– President Xi, this is a great honor for me. As you know, my research concerns the world's greatest civilizations and how they have evolved over time. What, for you, is the characteristic of Chinese society today that Europeans most frequently get wrong?

– Undoubtedly, the inner confidence that unites the whole population. You Westerners keep predicting that our system will soon implode, and yet it is yours that is in danger of showing cracks.

The internal market and inner confidence

– Where does this inner confidence come from?

– From our young people and from our domestic market. You Westerners don't realize that, in China, there are more people in the 20-35 age group than in any other. Month after month, it is they –these only children –who are seeing China take the lead over the USA in the consumer goods sector. Today, almost 25 million cars are sold in China every year, twice as many as in the USA, and it is the Chinese younger generation that will decide the norms for electric cars of the future. In telecommunications, Europe is attempting to postpone the adoption of 5G for another three to five years, whereas, by the summer of 2020, we already had over 100 million subscribers. For young Chinese people, the growth of the domestic market is the best proof of China's return to the world stage. They are the ones who now have the most say in the development of new smartphones with different video features. "I shop, therefore I am" is at the root of Chinese confidence in the future.

– A root that seems to me be to be crassly materialistic! And, what's more, how can you, as the leader of the country, guard against the danger of cyclical turnarounds that could put your theory in jeopardy?

– That's exactly what your compatriots still haven't grasped. The reason why we've chosen this sector is because our development on the home front is far from having reached its limit. Consumption accounts for less than 50% of GDP, as opposed to 70% in your country. We have almost $25,000 billion of bank deposits, i.e. over 150% of our GDP, mostly made up of private savings that parents and grandparents are now putting at the disposal of their only child or grandchild. Our Chinese millennials are staying single for longer and longer. 70% of them have owned an apartment since they were born. They all have smartphones and are beginning not to want a car that pollutes. Their real disposable income is twice that of Westerners with comparable salaries. So, the Chinese domestic market is nowhere near slowing down, and inner confidence is not waning. We say that 50% of the population live in urban areas, but this percentage is artificially high because of 200 million migrants. So our reservoir for any future growth is much bigger than it is generally perceived to be, if you consider that an urban dweller spends 3.4 times as much as someone living in a rural area. For instance, only 21 large groups producing consumer goods – eight of which are Western, by the way – have more than 100 million customers in China. You can see there's still some way to go.

– Even so, I don't quite see how you can build such confidence when I read in the press that 600 million of your citizens still only have an income of $150 a month.

– That's precisely what has surprised us as well over the last two years: e-commerce internet platforms like Meituan-Dianping and Pinduoduo, have both had a phenomenal success. They decided to focus on cities that rank second – that belong to what we call Tier 3, 4 or 5 – where hidden savings have turned out to be far greater than expected. Their success, too, has been far greater than expected and is reflected in their incredible market valuation – over $100 billion! It all goes to show that the wealth accumulated by Chinese families over time is far more than official statistics say.

– So, when it comes to judging the social climate, whereas we in the West look at the opinion polls, you look at retail sales. Is that it?

– Your opinion polls are never reliable – just look at the surprise election of Donald Trump in 2016. I look at the sales of baiju; that's the best indicator of any weakness.

– Your sales of what?

– Baiju. It's our national liquor. I would willingly offer you a glass, but I'm afraid it might affect the rest of our discussion. Every year, 1.2 billion nine-liter crates are sold; that's more than global sales of whisky, vodka, gin, rum and tequila put together. It's a huge market today of almost $85 billion, dominated by Kweichow Moutai, the market leader and leading world brand. It is so well-known that it gave rise to one of our most popular Chinese sayings: "People who drink Mouati don't need to buy it; those who buy it don't get the chance to taste it." More generally speaking, we Chinese keep a sharp lookout for all the festival days during the year that have commercial possibilities. There's only one festival every year when you Italian Catholics open your purses to give presents, and that's Christmas. We have one every month – twelve occasions every year when we Chinese show our love of celebrations. There is the New Year at the beginning of the year, various Valentine's Days, the 18th June organized by the distributor JD.com, our National Day in October, the Singles Festival on 11th November, etc. etc. Each one is an occasion to measure how much progress our country has made since the previous year.

– Unfortunately, Italians no longer have the means to give presents to their partners every month... Italian men used to give presents to women all the time but...

– Ah, women! Now there's another thing the West doesn't know about Chinese society. Women are the real hidden strength of China. Did you know that, in China, 60% of start-ups are founded by women, whereas it's only 20% in the USA? Or that 60% of e-warriors addicted to video fighting games are in fact women?

– Well, when I saw the tremendous *Change Destiny* campaign launched a few years ago in Shanghai by the cosmetics company SK II, I saw how a new generation of women were changing the position of women in society. It showed single women asserting their independence – so different from their traditional status as women who had been "left on the shelf".

– In China today, there are more women millionaires than men. The chairwoman of Gree Electric, Dong Mingzhu, nicknamed "Sister Dong", is a role model for all young Chinese women who want to be entrepreneurs. Let me remind you that 10,000 start-ups are founded every day in China, as opposed to only 1,000 in the USA. Time is on our side.

– And I had this image in my head of shy young Chinese women who needed platform heels to make them look taller – like the Spice Girls!

The real Chinese dictator: the young consumer

– Our young women have a lot of surprises in store for you. Now, although we're not going to talk politics today, I would like to admit something: that China is indeed a dictatorship, but the dictator is not "Uncle Xi", it's the young Chinese consumer.

– And yet, you have so many old people in your country and your population will age quickly over the next decade.

– Except, from an economic point of view, we are the youngest country in the world. Deloitte predicts that, by 2025, almost 50% of the population's disposable income will be in the hands of millennials and zoomers – Generation Z, now aged 10-15. Alimama, the data analysis subsidiary of Alibaba, estimates that Generation Z already accounts for 30% of the volume of purchases on its platform. If you are the head of global marketing for a brand, no major country is as young as China. The average age today of a buyer for cosmetics is 28 in China, as compared to 45 in Europe.

– In the West, we also live under a dictatorship – the dictatorship of brands that strive to maintain customer loyalty over time. You say it is young people who hold sway in China, and yet they have an average attention span of 8 seconds when it comes to videos on social media. Could it be that they are becoming less and less loyal to you?

– That is a big concern of mine, of course. It is the young people who constantly make me look towards the future and not be nostalgic for the past. Every morning, I have the impression I'm going duck shooting – which involves not aiming your gun at the place where the duck is now, but at where it will be when it takes wing. My task is made much easier because of my painful experience of the Cultural Revolution; the effect of that is to make me turn more towards the future than the past. For a young Chinese person, history is old and the future is young!

– I'm sure you know my friend Remo Ruffini, the brilliant chairman and CEO of Moncler. He has revolutionized marketing in the luxury sector, drawing on the example of the Villa Medici in Rome where, since the time of Louis xiv, France has invited young artists to spend a year there. Following this example, Remo has broken the code of the industry and, every month, invites a new designer to relook the down jackets Moncler is famous for, and adapt them to his or her own taste. The stores have become an addiction for your young people, who come back every month… and yet 90% of them still continue to buy from the traditional collection. Invite Remo to lunch and you'll find out how to tame your "young dictators"!

– Professor, I am a great admirer of Italian creativity; it's a field in which your global leadership is unrivalled. But the challenge facing me goes further than that. The L'Oréal cosmetics group can explain better than I can the way generations are changing so quickly. For the generation born in the 60s and 70s, it was all about "fight for the family/save your money". For the post-1980 generation, it was "assert yourself in front of others/run up debts". Then came the post-1990 generation who wanted to "live my life/celebrate the quality of experience", and finally, those born after 2000 proclaim, "We are the future/Chinese pride is the greatest". And now, there seems to be a new generation of "young dictators" every five years with new aspirations that I am supposed to react to.

– Your problem is that their means of communication keeps changing. In the West, the "Instabrand" on Instagram has replaced text by video. In China, Douyin – that we know as TikTok in the West – has abandoned micro-blogging on Twitter in favor of micro-videos, which are only just beginning to invade Europe.

– At my age, it's no easy matter to keep up with all this. It's easier in Europe where there has been no thrust given to innovation since the average purchasing power of households reached a plateau in 2012, after the euro crisis. In China, it's quite the contrary: I have to face new requests all the time from young people who are increasingly demanding, and increasingly finicky with regard to their needs. They attach a great deal of importance to the quality of the air and the water; they want personalized food products, based on DNA analysis; they reject some of the previous generation's consumer habits and consumer goods: beers, diapers, cereals, yoghurt, soap, fabric softeners, the bank branches, department stores, golf, diamonds, cars, oil, etc. etc. And while one has to deal with so much rejection, there is the reverse side of the coin: an apparently boundless creativity is developing – mergers between different sectors of markets that have already been penetrated, so as to create new market spaces and a new "experience".

– Yes, the famous Blue Ocean strategy, as the specialists call it. Like "skintertainment", a combination of cosmetics and entertainment which can end up – as it has in China – with marketing lipstick for men! We don't have that in the West!

– Cosmetics is a sector that has a lot of surprises in store for us because, according to experts at the Morgan Stanley investment bank, the premium sector only accounts for about a third of demand in China, whereas it is 50% in more developed countries like South Korea, Japan and the USA.

– What strikes me in what you say is this *élan* you feel among your young people. It's quite the opposite of the extremely conservative revolution that we are witnessing among our Western millennials. The criticisms they have of my generation are in fact very anti-*soixante-huitard*, as my French friends would say: respect for the environment, the search for meaning, a good balance between one's working life and family life, and the quality of life. Such aspirations amount to a return to traditional values. These millennials are in fact paying tribute to the wise but apocryphal aphorism attributed to Mark Twain "The two most important days of your life are the day you were born and the day you find out why."

– You're lucky to have them! I only wish I had young people like yours – mine are much too demanding, asking for the "ME to WE", that is to say, they want satisfaction from a product or an experience that is not only personal but which also benefits their entourage!

– The quest for personal happiness is as old as the hills. I am doing research into how happiness can be experienced at societal level. In this respect, I would be most interested to know what your scheme of things is for the future.

– My answer is this: social ranking.

"Long live social commerce!"

– Could you explain exactly what social ranking is, please? I have to say that, for a European like me, it seems like a scary reminder of the Big Brother scenario. I saw in the press that the internet giant Tencent was going to use its social media WeChat to categorize all of its billion users for you, on the basis of five criteria: honor, security, wealth, consumption and sociability. For a European, this has a whiff of the Stasi in East Germany!

– I am delighted that you don't understand, because this means we can look further into the gap between China and the West. The way the Chinese regard this ranking is very different from yours. Bear in mind that we have a tradition of building up a network of relationships – *guanxi* – and this is a Chinese person's most precious possession. Whereas you in the West look on your professional career as a series of promotions linked to salary rises, the main objective of Chinese people, throughout their lives, will be to extend their network of relationships. This will enable them to steer their way through what they foresee as being an extremely fluid system.

– But what has this to do with social ranking?

– The aim is to build up for each Chinese person, a virtual

community of about 200 people – the equivalent of your "Friends and Family" – with whom he or she shares the same tastes and aspirations. In this way, a virtual link is created to fill the vacuum left behind by the decline of the family. And, since my people are very pragmatic, they will be all the more attracted by this system if they can gain a tangible advantage from it – social commerce.

– And what is this social commerce?

– It's a new form of commerce that we have invented to make group commerce cost-effective. The Groupon company attempted to promote it in the West, with only limited success. It was you, in the West, who initiated online commerce – e-commerce – through the internet, and made a fortune for Amazon. In China, we began with m-commerce by cellphone, made possible by the Alipay and WeChat-Pay payment systems. But these purchases were always individual. Social commerce is the online version of Western-style shopping, with its social entertainment dimension. A social media platform like WeChat brings together a community of young people – very often young women – who watch a KOL – a Key Opinion Leader – on live streaming. He or she presents a whole range of products to buy, in a fun way. Whereas Western e-commerce focuses on buying things for everyday life and offers practical solutions, social commerce generates the same pleasurable feelings as shopping and helps create a new social link that engenders new virtual encounters. What looks like Big Brother to you is in fact a new source of "Friends and Family" for me.

– Very clever! And is this gaining ground?

– It has been stupendously successful! We had estimated that social commerce, which accounted for 8% of e-commerce in 2017, would double to at least 15% by 2022, but the Covid-19 crisis has speeded up the trend. With regard to luxury goods, a study carried out by the Union of Swiss Banks estimated that a KOL's influence could account for 40% of any decision to purchase, whereas the brand name itself, even if it were a century old, only had a 30% influence on the decision. So the editor of *Vogue China* has more followers than the magazine itself.

– I have indeed observed the boom in "social beauty" – a key segment of the cosmetics sector. The 2.8 billion users of social media send each other almost 2,000 billion selfies every year. It shows that they are attaching more and more importance to the image they want to project in their online lives.

– And there has been an explosion in virtual gifts too. Perhaps I could offer you some Louis Vuitton armor for your avatar in your favorite video game?

– That's very nice of you, but I think I'd rather keep my Prada dress.

– Did you know that you can now buy a dress like that in China for no more than it would cost in Italy? When you fly back home, make a stop-over on Hainan island. It has just been declared a totally duty-free area and is going to become a "must visit" in China. Shenzhen was Deng Xiaoping's brainchild; mine is going to be Hainan.

– Perhaps Sanya – the Rimini of Hainan – could take its inspiration from the Museum of Ice Cream in San Francisco where visitors can pose for selfies against the most improbable backdrops and use them to enrich their online lives. In a way, Netflix, which has revolutionized VOD, shares your approach, because it identifies 2,000 "taste clusters" among its target population, so it can tailor its movies to demand.

– So, isn't Netflix manipulating opinion more than our CCP?

– The difference is that you say you want to extend this principle to every aspect of daily life and, for a European, this is rather frightening.

– True. We don't only want to organize entertainment, but to organize social life as a whole, beginning with family life. Why should this be frightening?

"Gucci is an attitude"

– You surely can't mean you want to invent virtual families?

– That's exactly what one of the aims is. One of my country's main weaknesses could well be its demography. The problem is not that our population is ageing – a fact that is greatly exaggerated in the West. We will never be faced with your pension problem because – Confucius be praised! – the older generation in China will keep working until they die. They know that work means health, and I don't have to remind you that, when Bismarck invented retirement at the age of 65, life expectancy was only 55 years. The most fundamental problem is the low birth rate, even after the end of the single child policy in 2017. There were only 17 million births in 2017 and 15 million in 2019, whereas the official target was 20 million. The main obstacle is the limited financial means of young couples; in spite of their parents' and grandparents' savings, they can't afford a second child. We are going to remedy this, for I am determined not to end up like Japan where 40% of young people are still "virgins" at the age of 34!

"I hate my family"

– But with a bunch of only children who can't play as a team, you're never going to beat us at football! As any good

Italian will insist, the family is the main foundation stone of society. Now, out of all the countries in the world, ours are undoubtedly the two that attach the most importance to the nuclear family. Without that, you run the risk of people feeling isolated and, if you put this together with the frantic gregariousness of social media, it could be extremely dangerous.

– Absolutely! That's exactly where the whole problem lies for me. Today, the Chinese family with a single child is seen as a real burden: the "1-2-4" of "one child, two parents and four grandparents". This feeling is strengthened by the generation gap introduced by the internet, which makes parents look more like grandparents. So, at the present time, the family – the backbone of any young person in China – is becoming dislocated. And this is why the number of pet dogs and cats is increasing by almost 15% a year in cities. 88% of the owners are women, half of whom are single.

– Hmm. Cats may well be very effective when it comes to selling things on Instagram, but they aren't going to make it possible for you to make yourself the leading power in the world. I had a fascinating talk with Alessandro Michele, a brilliant man who was behind the resurrection of the Gucci brand a few years ago. He quadrupled turnover in four years, raising it to almost €8 billion, and raised Gucci to the same level as Hermès, Louis Vuitton and Chanel. Alessandro talked to me about the ad which showed a Chinese grandfather and his grandson, both wearing Gucci suits with flower patterns, and both smiling. The slogan proclaimed, "Gucci is an attitude". Alessandro explained that he had identified the need to fill the vacuum felt by Chinese millennials by means of a new family that the Gucci brand could provide. He was the first one to realize that your young people, who account for 60% of the buyers of certain items in the brand's product range, wanted to acquire a substitute family more than they wanted to access Western culture. Hence the subtle use of an Italian background – in only black and white – that made the foreground stand out with the flashy colors of the new Chinese energy, represented by a grandfather and a little brother that all Chinese millennials dream of having.

– Alessandro Michele was very clever: he made the European legacy relevant to Chinese modernity.

– In the same way, the Christian Dior brand took the risk of choosing a young Chinese woman, Angelababy, for its ambassador. Although she is a product of plastic surgery and her intellectual capacities are far below those of the brand's ambassadors in the West, she is seen as "aspirational" and "approachable", a contradiction that appeals to a generation that likes to play with paradoxes. You see how bringing our cultures closer together produces a win-win situation.

– That's what impresses me most about your Western brands. I sometimes have the impression that they understand what makes our young people tick better than we do as Chinese leaders. And I have to make sure our young people don't slip away from us.

The triumph of virtual hybridity

– They won't slip away from you if you take your inspiration from Gucci's unprecedented success. Alessandro Michele likes to underline the importance of the notion of "hybridity' in our lives. He plays on the amazing faculty of his female customers to combine magnificent Gucci blouses with classic jeans. Young Chinese women must be able to find their own hybridity in order to blossom. Fashion will provide them with the means of showing their peaceful rebellion, wearing Doc Martens, just as the punkettes did in London back in the 1970s.

– Peaceful rebellion… A nice phrase, but it will have to be controlled, even so. Are you asking me to think about the possibilities of virtual hybridity?

– Once again, look at the luxury industry. Take the example of the French LVMH group. Its former digital director, Ian Rogers, has said that the internet has redefined the notion of "local", the roots we are all attached to. Because of the internet, "near home" has now become "shared interests", as is the case of photos on Instagram that are "liked". If you are a young person in China, you want to invent your own virtual hybridity and get the feeling that you are combining real life and virtual life into something that corresponds to your aspirations.

– I've already noticed this with young people who spend the evening in their room. They have three cellphones: one for a TV series, a second for a video game and a third for live streaming – the reality video-show they watch with their social community. And that could be a marvelous opportunity for China to lead the world, through the video games industry. It could become the mainstay of our virtual hybridity and the flagship of Chinese culture. It's a $150 billion market and, to my mind, it could topple the pay-TV market which is worth almost $300 billion and currently in American hands. Our video game developers are running neck and neck with our American competitors; they have 25% of the global market, but they are already leaders of the cellphone video games sector, which will be the future standard worldwide. Our giants Tencent and NetEase are already way ahead of Electronic Arts and Activation, and between a third and a half of developers of games for the West are already Chinese. In October 2019, Tencent's adaptation for cellphones of the Call of Duty game was downloaded by 100 million players in one week! To quote the words of Huang Zheng, the founder of Pinduoduo, the social commerce giant: "Reality has become virtual, and virtuality is a part of reality."

– That combination was beautifully illustrated in Beijing a few years ago when Japanese artists from TeamLab performed at the Pace Gallery in the "798" complex of the Dashanzi Art district. They video-projected waves of digital water-lilies over the whole gallery, clothing some young women dressed entirely in white in a moving mass of flowers. Their boyfriends immortalized the moment by taking photos. It was a much more exciting experience than one of those weekends in the countryside we so love in the West!

– This mixture of the real and the virtual worlds is something that Adrian Cheng sees in children under 10 – the "alpha generation". He is the head of the New World Group and the jewelry giant Chow Tai Fook and he told the *Financial Times*: "Alpha Gen are using these [video] games as a way to communication and socialize. […] They are used to the idea that they have a virtual self, an avatar, and that avatar has become a monetization tool. The avatar can go shopping in virtual malls and buy things. […] The Alpha Gen will buy these things to get a sense of definition and to get a sense of place within this world. " It is hardly surprising that these very new consumers spend on average six hours a day on the internet.

– I'm sorry to have to say this, but I would rather continue to live my life in "the most beautiful country in the world". This need to resort to the virtual world is completely foreign to me; real life gives me everything I need. And that was the message of the Zero Likes Given exhibition in New York in 2019, sponsored by Kahlua, the liqueur brand. The only exhibits were extremely moving photos that had never got any "likes" on Instagram. On leaving the exhibition, visitors were asked if they had ever missed out on any real sensation by giving preference to taking a selfie. That situation is symptomatic: your people are going to abandon their ability to make good judgments and succumb to the virtual "ideological isolation" of social media, which Barack Obama warned about.

– It's all too easy for Barack Obama to say that, but he did nothing during his terms of office to put the brakes on the Netflix algorithm – which determines 75% of the choices made by subscribers –, or on Amazon's algorithm, whose recommendations account for a third of purchases on its platform.

– For me, all that signifies more of a threat to our society's diversity than any promise of a rosy future. And, by the way, I hear that you have asked Chinese hospitals to accept only sperm that has "favorable political qualities". Isn't this approach going to lead you to everyone ending up looking the same?

– Professor, you forget that I have a country of 1.4 billion people to govern and, if you allow them to go where they want, they are the most undisciplined people in the world. That's what made Mao introduce the famous *hukou*, a residence permit limited to one province. Once again, bear in mind that 600 million of my fellow citizens still have very small incomes. Rather than pursue diversity in society, I have to concentrate on the emergence of a "Chinese dream" that will become a reality in the future.

The Chinese dream of "4.0 Marxism"

– A dream is always about satisfying an unfulfilled desire. From your point of view, what is your people's biggest dream ?

– Our greatest strength is something you have lost in Europe – a common objective shared by all. For us, it is a belief that, by 2049 – the hundredth anniversary of Mao's coming to power –, China will be leading the world. It is this belief that makes it possible for the present generation to accept the sacrifices demanded of them, because they know that their sacrifice will mean that their children will lead the world and have a real edge over the Americans.

– And, in your opinion, what is the worst threat that might stop this dream from coming true?

The "kingdom of extremes"

– My answer must never leave this room. The worst threat is social inequality. We have called ourselves the Middle Kingdom, but today, in fact, we are a "kingdom of extremes". According to the Hurun ranking of the wealthiest Chinese people, 2,000 Chinese own the equivalent of the UK's GDP. According the Farfetch company, the Chinese luxury market comprises only 7.6 million consumers.

– And according to McKinsey, only one million people account for half of all luxury expenditure!

– This is a real problem for our public finances, because only 28 million Chinese pay income tax, whereas, in theory, 190 million should be paying it. This means that income tax is only 8% of our tax revenue, as compared to 25% in OECD countries. The Chinese are used to extremes – for instance, we have an extreme climate with severe winters and extremely hot summers – but the problem is that the period we're living in doesn't improve matters.

– Obviously, if nothing is done about it, we are all set for unprecedented social tension. Remember what happened after the 2008 financial crisis: the whole world agreed on the need to put an end to the growth of inequality. But, in fact, monetary easing by the central banks only benefited the wealthy who, for the first time in their lives, could borrow money at zero interest. It's what we call "increased capital inequality". Added to this, over the next decade, we're going to see increased labor inequality generated by the artificial intelligence revolution, which will probably mean that 20% to 40% of jobs will be cut. So, we are facing a twofold inequality: in capital and labor. At the same time, all the major Western consultancy firms are talking about the rise to power of the Chinese middle classes, who represent 300 to 400 million future consumers. Do you really believe this is true?

– As usual, it's all a question of how you define your terms. According to the Hurun report of 2018, at that time there were only 33 million middle-class households in China if one used the Western definition with regard to income. In economic terms, the concept of middle class goes back to the USA in the second half of the 20th century, when it was defined as a family of two parents and two children living in a house with an average surface area of 240 square meters. Now a Chinese household is based on a single child and an apartment whose size, on average, corresponds to 15 square meters per person. Therefore, you can't expect the Chinese middle class to behave in the same way as the Western middle class.

– And, what's more, because of forced urbanization, your population density is much higher.

– Even if you take the example of Hong Kong, which is supposed to be partly influenced by the West, one out of every two inhabitants lives above the 16th floor, and the average monthly salary of 17,500 Hong Kong dollars hardly covers the average rent of 16,500 Hong Kong dollars for a single room. And, as a final point, the starting salary of a young university is only $800. Your so-called experts have to understand that their cut-and-paste approach is yet another example of ethnocentrism.

– But, when you're faced with an increase in inequality – as you anticipate –, how are you going to maintain the sense of the collective that has been the strength of your civilization? I am always struck by the fact that when you meet Chinese people, they introduce themselves by first giving their surname, and then their first name – it proves that community interest must always take precedence over the individual. But if you go down the path of pre-distribution of wealth – as has increasingly been the case in the USA in the Trump era and in other ossified Western countries – I can't see any glorious future in store for you!

– My response to the point that you have raised can be summed up in one word: "nationalism", the quintessence of the Chinese dream.

"La Dolce China"?

– The last time we were tempted by nationalism in Italy, it didn't end well, either for the country or for Mussolini – and I hope you don't meet the same end as he did. I don't need to remind you that half of your emperors didn't die of natural causes!

– The difference is that we Chinese believe that we have always had a heaven-blessed mission. Today, our mission is the need to invent a global way of life for a world of eight billion people, whilst Europe and the USA are still incapable of changing the habits of their 700 million privileged inhabitants. We in China have to invent a new nationalism as quickly as possible – "4.0 Marxism" –, based on a sharing economy created by means of digitalization. That is the only way to develop a cost structure and a use of natural resources that is in line with a growing world population. This new type of nationalism also means inventing new ways of life, including new ways of communicating. You still call us a "dictatorship" – by definition hostile to any new form of communication – and yet Western children aged 10 to 15 are thronging to TikTok, which was invented here by ByteDance. They want to communicate with each other via the new language of short videos – a language that we Chinese developed. This new nationalism is also the legitimate reconquest of our domestic market which we, more than any other nation, opened up to your Western companies in the past. So, for several years now, I have been pleased to see Chinese companies taking back market share in sectors as diverse as automobiles, detergents, beer, hygiene products and cosmetics. They have started to do so at the low end of the market, but I hope that, one day, they will also occupy the high end of it. What's more, this new nationalism will bring about China's return to the world stage in the healthcare sector – a sector in which the West has always scorned our traditional medicine.

– And yet, in 2016, the Food and Drug Administration approved – for the first time –a treatment derived from your traditional medicine.

– It was high time! We believe that a human being is not just a body; pain will go away more quickly if you treat the mind as well. Chinese medicine is based on a metaphysical view of the body in which a balance is to be found between the complementary principles of yin and yang. You have rejected our belief in the paths and flows of energy and have preferred an approach that is simply about engineering. We have a holistic approach to mind and body, whereas your philosophy reduces medicine to the study and treatment of each isolated part. Our medical advances in the next decade will surprise you, just as you will be surprised by the speed of our advances in internet-related media.

– Be careful, though, not to confuse nationalism and patriotism. General de Gaulle put it very well when he said that patriotism is when there is a prevalence of love among your fellow citizens; nationalism is when hatred of others predominates. If you are only motivated by nationalism, you will never manage to build a "*dolce China*" and very few Italians will envy your situation.

– I see nationalism more as something that cements society, replacing religion – whose ascent would be a threat to my country. Look at the Moslem world: today, we have a radical Islamism that took root when Arab nationalism collapsed after the Six-Day War in 1967, when Nasser lost all credibility vis-à-vis Israel. That was the moment when the Arab world began to sink into despair and a number of Moslems took refuge in radicalization. This is what I have to avoid in our country.

– But religion doesn't necessarily lead to radicalization. Remember your private hour-and-a-half interview with the Archbishop of Canterbury when you visited England. I see Europe more as a potential source of inspiration for you, and for your young people. They may well be delighted at the prospect of your "Chinese dream", but I'm sure that, above all, they would like to be among the 500,000 students who get the chance to study abroad. And "abroad" will increasingly mean Europe if, following in the steps of Donald Trump, the USA continues to close its doors to them.

Help! Europe, I can't breathe!

– Yes, it's true that, for our students, the vicarious pleasures of the West play a part in the "Chinese dream".

– You should listen to your millennials when they talk about their criteria for choosing a tourist destination: it's all about nature, security and food. Your Gen Z is the same as in the rest of the world. Their list of priorities are the recent public health crisis, security, authentic produce, healthcare, respect for the environment and lifestyle. And it's in Europe, not in the USA, that they're going to find their inspiration. In a word, they just want to breathe.

– I do realize that the Covid-19 crisis has underlined the fact that the imbalances related to our growth must be corrected. We get the message, and have been the first to react to this.

– Take the example of food – it's a subject that our two countries share a passion for. The food sector needs a complete rethink, and we should collaborate much more on this. The multinational food companies are ripe for some disruption, just like the technology companies in the 1970s, the financial sector in the 1980s, and the communications industry in the first decade of this century. According to the *Financial Times*, the food industry has seriously under-invested in technology. Globally, only between eight and ten billion dollars are invested in AgTech every year. The result is that, today, it takes eight apples to produce the same number of calories as one apple did in 1960. In 1940, it took only one calory of fossil fuel to produce 2.4 nutritional calories;

today it takes from 7 to 10 to produce only one! On a global scale, it is estimated that 10% of food produced is modified or contaminated, and 30% is wasted. This is the third largest source of CO_2 emissions. The products most likely to get spoiled are milk, olive oil, fish, coffee and orange juice. And then there is the water problem, which I'm sure you're aware of, since you have spent the astronomical sum of $48 billion on diverting part of the Yangzi Jiang river in order to prevent water shortages in Beijing.

– In what way do you think Europe could be a source of inspiration in this field?

– Stop looking systematically towards the USA for inspiration. Can you honestly find answers in a country where Donald Trump's daily diet consists of burgers, fries and Coca-Cola? The most reputable investor in the USA, Warren Buffet, learned that to his cost when he had to write-down Kraft Heinz by $15 billion. Even financiers get indigestion from junk food! Look rather at the UK, where the authorities aim to reduce the excessive calory content of processed foods by 20%. You have 120 million diabetics in China, so there is an urgent need here for this sort of thing. And look at the French company Mérieux Nutrisciences which specializes in food safety and is trying to do the impossible in a country where barely 11% of the population say they trust food brands and only 45% say they are willing to spend more on healthier foods. Go and meet the members of the Rethink X Team think tank who are confident that a new model of "Food as a Service" can be invented, notably thanks to future advances in precision biology that can cause micro-organisms to develop complex organic molecules. In this way, by 2030, the cost of producing protein by precision fermentation could be five times less than normal animal protein, and ten times less by 2035. My friend Vitalino Fiorillo from Bocconi University is a food expert and he predicts that, whereas "up to now, products have been designed for the European consumer, then exported to Asia; in the future, it will be the opposite." You see, even my country is ready to collaborate!

– I am well aware of the fact that, from the time of the French Revolution up to the Arab Spring, popular uprisings have often had their roots in the rising food prices.

– The problem for us in the West is rather that, for 40 years, we have seen falling food prices, which means that we spend only 10% of our income on food now, whereas it was 30% two generations ago. On the other hand, our expenditure on housing has risen from 10% to 30% of our budget, sometimes even rising to 50% in large cities.

– This is why we have to collaborate and invent new food models based on nutritional value that can maximize the positive effects of organic produce, which produces returns of less than 30% and has the disadvantage of costing up to twice as much to produce.

– Anyway, there is no way we can stay in a situation in which 75% of our calorie intake depends on only twelve types of plants and five types of animals.

– With pigs at the top of the list in China! Every Chinese person eats on average a hundred grams of pork a day, which is the equivalent of half a pig per year per person. But you will never make pork any less popular – it's a national institution. To show you just how much of an institution it is, let me tell you about the day when the Mayor of Shanghai introduced garbage recycling – between kitchen waste, plastics, harmful waste and recyclables. The first weeks produced disastrous results because people had trouble understanding these new concepts. So, with a stroke of genius, the City Council changed the name of the categories, making them much more pragmatic: "What pigs like / What pigs don't like / What can kill pigs / What enables you to buy a pig." Since then, recycling has worked beautifully!

– This leads me on quite nicely to the cultural sphere. Let's start with art. We Europeans have a lot we can help you with. Gong Yan, curator of the Power Station of Art in Shanghai said herself: "China needs art, for we are too passive; we have forgotten our brains, we are afraid of emotions."

– You are right to point this out, but I can assure you I already have a plan for this area – a plan to revive the past glory of China.

– Oh dear, I fear that you are on the way to making the same mistake that Napoleon III made in France almost two centuries ago. Like you, he wanted his own style to be a legacy he would leave to posterity, a style inspired by his country's past glory. It turned out to be *l'art pompier* – academic art – examples of which all French people dread finding among the belongings left to them by their great aunts. On the other hand, the art that has stood the test of time is that of rebels – the Impressionists – an art as revolutionary as the Industrial Revolution of the time. They paved the way for Art Nouveau and for the modernist movements that enabled European culture to reach its heights. Don't make the same mistake as Napoleon III. Yes, let your artists take their inspiration from their Chinese roots, but, above all, encourage them to bring those roots up to date and into the era of the artificial intelligence revolution. And let them travel the world in search of other sources of inspiration. I have no doubt that they will find European sources most refreshing. They will have the same reaction as James Salter who wrote in his memoirs, *Burning the Days*: "What Europe finally gave me was education, not school lessons, but something more elevated, a view of existence: how to have leisure, love, food and conversation; how to look at nakedness, architecture, streets – all new and seeking to be thought of in a different way."

– I like your idea of a sort of "Xi Jinping Art Nouveau". As you know, we have built more museums since the year 2000 than were built during the 19th and 20th centuries put together. As a good many of them are empty, we could fill them with this type of Art Nouveau. This interview has also given me the idea for a museum of European civilization in Beijing, which could then have branches in the provinces, beginning here in Shanghai on the West Bund. It would certainly be in our common interest to bring our two ancient civilizations together. This museum could represent my vision of the 21st century in which a closer relationship with Europe would also make it possible for us, in turn, to influence you. We could call it the "Museum of EuraXia" to echo of the way I see Eurasia in the future. Yes, an excellent idea! If only for that suggestion, I must thank you for this conversation. And, as a sign of my gratitude, please accept this bottle of vintage Maotai. I hope that, when you drink it with your husband and friends back in Italy, you will raise a toast to China! But – a piece of friendly advice – have a good mouthful of pasta after each shot! But now, it's time for you to visit the museum. I hope you enjoy it!

4

Wednesday – Emeishan (Sichuan), Lord Fitzbacon

"What's ours is ours. What's yours is negotiable."
Nikita Khrushchev

– Thank you, Lord Fitzbacon, for having made the trip out to this remote part of Sichuan, famous now for two things. First of all, Mount Emei, that you can see from here and is one of the four sacred Buddhist mountains in China. Secondly, this ultramodern distillery, built by the highly-regarded Chinese architecture firm Neri & Hu for your Scottish friends from the Pernod-Ricard group. They're going to make the first Chinese malt whiskey. It will be an iconic product and I am determined that sales of it will very soon better those of its Japanese equivalents. I thought this would be the perfect place to talk about global geopolitics in the future, because it's a good illustration of what our two countries can accomplish when they combine their know-how. Since I suspect that lunches in the House of Lords fill up your diary much more than your stomach, I have arranged for a tasting of our first distillates after our interview. They still need a little time to mature, rather like the relationship between our two countries. I say this because, after a rare upturn a few years ago when David Cameron was in Downing Street, our relations have since become more distant. But I'd like to think that this will not affect the fullness of our exchanges.

– President Xi, I very much appreciate your initiative, particularly since I feel that history is gathering speed. The choices we make in the coming years will be crucial for the

21st century. And, of course, one of the key issues is the part that your country will play.

The re-Orientation of the 21st century

– For us in China, there are no two ways about it. My friend Ren Zhengfei, the CEO of the Huawei Group, puts it very well: "The wheel of history is turning". And it can't be stopped. The 21st century will mark the return of Asia and, in particular, the return of China. The fact that we faded into the background between 1850 and 1978 will soon be seen as just a blip in our long history.

When *sharp power* gets the better of *soft power*

– But that's not going to be easy. One has to avoid upsetting the delicate balance of our world.

– What are you afraid of? Kishore Mahbubani, the founding Dean of the Lee Kuan Yew School of Public Policy, has explained very clearly why Asian governance is superior to yours: it all stems from the fact that, in the USA, since Ronald Reagan, we have seen that "government is the problem". This has contributed to the decline in the quality of the politicians who have been our discussion partners, right up to Donald Trump; who applied himself most professionally to bringing the process to an end. During the same period, Asia's competency has gradually established itself – in its respect for science and technology, in its culture of pragmatism, and in its will to learn the best global practices. And all this combined with its extremely strong motivation on the part of Asia to catch up on the West and reduce the gap between them.

– The problem is not so much your return to the world stage as the fact that you only go by international rules when it suits you, and this will never allow any solid foundations to be laid. As one of our most brilliant minds, Oscar Wilde, said over a century ago: "In all important matters, style, not sincerity, is the essential."

– If I remember rightly, Oscar Wilde is buried in France, which probably explains why your French partners often remind us not to trust British sincerity. And yet, I don't see why our approach should shock you. Our model has been tried and tested: "the Singapore model at home, the American model for abroad". So, at home, we have a modern economy under the careful management of a single party; abroad, we have international norms that, above all, reflect our interests. You tolerate the Singapore and US systems, so why take offence at ours?

– Because you only see international relations in terms of power politics, which precludes the building up of any lasting relationship.

– But wasn't this already the case in the 19th century with Theodore Roosevelt and the Monroe Doctrine which brought American influence to bear on Cuba, the Philippines, Guam, Panama, Alaska and Venezuela, at the expense of Spain, Canada and your United Kingdom? The problem today is not so much that we have recourse to "sharp power", but that you allowed yourself to be seduced by the dangerous attractions of the USA and its "soft power" in the second half of the 20th century.

– Oscar Wilde would have far preferred soft power!

– Except that you can't ask the Chinese to excel in matters of seduction. Our cultures are different. Traditionally, when a European man wants to ask for a woman's hand in marriage, he gives her a bunch of nine of the most beautiful and most fragrant roses he can find. A Chinese man will probably present her with a bouquet of 1,000 plastic roses, so as to take her breath away slightly and show her who is going to be the boss in the marriage. However, this doesn't stop us from getting what we want by devious means. Have you read what Amélie Nothomb wrote? "China is like a wily courtesan who can make people forget her innumerable physical imperfections without even concealing them, and this causes her lovers to become infatuated with her."

– But that doesn't work, because every Chinese family is a matriarchal structure.

– One point to you. Yes, it is women who really govern everyday life in China.

– I can assure you, it's the same thing in my country where Maggie Thatcher is still a national icon. It was she who had the brilliant idea of negotiating with Deng Xiaoping over the "one country, two systems" principle which would operate in Hong Kong for 50 years. She was convinced that two successive generations couldn't make the same mistake, and that Hong Kong's capitalism would end up taking over your country. It would only take a few years. Conversely, in Hong Kong, you have just violated an international treaty by imposing your National Security law, in order to get total control over the territory. I am a great believer in what René Char said: "When you act, be like a savage; when you plan, be like a strategist." When history judges you, Maggie Thatcher will be the strategist, you will be the savage.

Hong Kong: "two countries, one system"

– I was sure this subject would come up in our discussion and I am delighted to be able to deal with it straight away. First of all, the action we took was totally legal, because the

1984 treaty, through Hong Kong's "Basic Law", provided for the introduction of a National Security law. But the Hong Kong government never introduced one. You must admit that if, after 23 years, one of your Lords had not done his job as a law-maker and proposed a bill in due time, you would feel free to act without asking for his opinion. Furthermore, the way I see it, the people of Hong Kong did not revolt for political reasons but for economic ones, as is the case in most large-scale popular uprisings. History shows that, from the French Revolution up to the Arab Spring, the trigger has generally been rising food prices. In this case, we were facing hyperinflation but, for the first time, it was in the real estate sector as a result of American monetary easing. Real estate prices had doubled in under 10 years, which effectively meant that young Hong Kong residents were being deprived of their right to housing, and money was going in the pockets of a dozen or so tycoons who couldn't care less about social cohesion. So, we were justified in intervening, to make the economy able to prosper once again – in peace.

– The inflation in real estate prices was principally the result of the fact that, for 20 years, under pressure from local tycoons, the Hong Kong government stopped providing the extra 50,000 units of social housing every year that we had allowed for when we left in 1997. This was made worse by the arrival of 50,000 mainlanders in Hong Kong every year. The solution to the problem would have been to rework social housing policy, not to deprive people of their freedom!

– I like to say that freedom is not inherited, it is earned. It can't derive from some contract that is over 20 years old and that refers to a hitherto untested regime. It must come from a forward-looking project, and the Hong Kong opposition has never come up with one. Hong Kong should have been a model for the mainland as a whole; as one of the most densely-populated urban areas in the world, it should have invented the smart city. But nothing has happened. Conversely, our intervention will enable Hong Kong to reinvent itself.

– And lose its rule of law? It was precisely this rule of law that made it unique in the region. With almost a quarter of global GDP less than a four-hour flight away, it was the only place where a dependable contract could be signed. And all that is going to disappear because of your intervention.

– I believe the opposite. I think Hong Kong is going to surprise you and reinvent itself in the coming years. Besides, we are always delighted when one of your British "buddies" sells his house or sells his shares on the Hong Kong stock exchange, because that gives us the chance to buy them at a giveaway price. We can do this through the South Connect procedure that we set up a few years ago to enable people from the Mainland to invest on the Hong Kong stock exchange. Their investments already account for about 15% of the volume of trade on the Hong Kong stock exchange. The Hang Seng Index has recently been trading below its book value – at the price of mere ink and paper – something that has only happened three times in over 20 years. So, at those prices, we're only too happy to show our confidence in the future of the "Fragrant Harbor".

– And what new foundations is this promised prosperity going to be built on?

– On reinvented versions of the city's three traditional supports. First of all, finance. We are going to repatriate the head offices of our best companies to Hong Kong. In the past, these companies had no other choice than to go looking for capital in the USA. Our exceptional future economic growth will enable Hong Kong to attract capital from the whole world over. Secondly, corporate services. We're going to extend them to the Greater Bay Area, to the Guangdong region, just north of the city – it has 80 million inhabitants who are preparing to make it the California of the 21st century. Ten years from now, this region will have a GDP the equivalent of Germany's. Thirdly, tourism. It will no longer be centered on luxury goods that, from now on, you'll be able to buy on the mainland for the same price; it will focus on a cultural package celebrating the long and glorious history of our civilization, and on wide-ranging healthcare that our people now go to Bangkok or Seoul to obtain.

– You're just reversing the equation: your "one country, two systems" is going to become "two countries, one system". In late 2019, BBC surveys showed that only 10% of the local population felt Chinese, and this sank to a mere 5% of 18-to-29-year-olds. How are you going to weld together the two populations – of Hong Kong and the Mainland?

– Please, let's not get things out of proportion here. At the present time, Hong Kong's GDP accounts for only 3% of that of Mainland China. This isn't 1997 anymore.

– But Hong Kong bank assets are eight times the local GNP – 25% of Mainland GDP. Stop claiming that you can do without Hong Kong; it's still a major source of finance for you.

– We don't destroy things if they work in our favor. In the first stage, Hong Kong will be a sort of heterogeneous combination of, on the one hand, London and its investment bankers and, on the other hand, Monaco and its wealthy retirees. You'll see… time will work in our favor.

– Personally, I fear that this will damage your image throughout the world for a long time to come, and will penalize you in your expansion plans here, there and everywhere. I think you're far too optimistic. Don't just take my word for it; remember what Billy Wilder said: "The optimists died in the gas chambers; the pessimists have pools in Beverley Hills."

– You can keep your Hollywood – it's a thing of the past! And let me remind you that China has never invaded anyone.

– That was true until you started the "New Silk Roads" initiative.

The "New Silk Rout?"

– Our "New Silk Roads" are in no way an invasion. On the contrary, they are an opportunity to help almost half the world to speed up its development – something the World Bank has failed lamentably to do since it was founded, and whose very existence was justified by this objective. When I came to power in 2012, our balance of payments showed a large annual surplus of several hundred billion dollars, notably because of the increasing trade surplus with the USA. In the first decade of this century, my predecessors saw fit to reinvest this money into US Treasury bills, to the tune of an astronomical $1,300 billion. The 2008 crisis taught us the cruel lesson that this vendor financing would never be reimbursed. This gave me the idea of proposing to friendly countries – mainly in Asia, Africa and Eastern Europe – that they should replicate our 40-year success in terms of development: public infrastructures would be built at very favorable terms, complemented by private entrepreneurial initiatives. The response was so enthusiastic that we then had the idea of formalizing our approach under the name BRI – the Belt Road Initiative – and with institutions like the AIIB, the Asian Infrastructure Investment Bank.

– Unfortunately, the idyllic picture you paint doesn't stand up to objective analysis. For a start, on the pretext of helping these countries, you have often pushed them into the "debt trap", as in the case of Djibouti where, over a period of two years, you lent it the equivalent of 75% of its GDP; or the Maldives, which is now barely solvent. In Malaysia, your investment in rail transportation – over $20 billion – has had to be cancelled by the new government, following suspicions of corruption. You have taken the same approach as you did before with rare earths – key elements needed for the miniaturization of electronics in consumer goods. You hold about 30% of the world's deposits of rare earths and, because of environmental issues, the USA and Europe have stopped production of them. This has meant that, for certain mineral ores, you control as much as 50% of global production. And you frequently use this as leverage in negotiations. With Japan, for instance, you want to place restrictions on their imports of rare earths so that this benefits "Made in China".

– What I hear in your words is the bitterness of the colonists of yesteryear who saw the New World slipping through their fingers. We have no desire at all for hegemony; our priorities have always been purely domestic.

– But the fact is that your "BRI" program is so lacking in transparency that it's really difficult to discern the breadth of it. In 2019, he Jamestown Foundation estimated your aggregate outlay on the "New Silk Roads" at $415 billion for the building of infrastructures, and $250 billion for other types of investment. But, since 2019, your largesse has been considerably reduced because of pressure on your own balance of payments and the disastrous financial results of your ventures. In Pakistan, for example, according to Bloomberg, only $19 billion were spent instead of the intended $60 billion, as a result of your problems with the port and airport infrastructures around Gwadar. It's estimated that you have already defaulted on 30% of all your loans. This is hardly surprising when you think that, out of the 78 countries chosen, 27 are considered junk and 14 are not even ranked by the various agencies. And your attempt to bring Italy into the "New Silk Roads" isn't going to change matters. What's more, your much-vaunted Asian Infrastructure Investment Bank announced grandly that it was capitalized at $100 billion which, with leverage, gives it a strike power of $250 billion. Up to now, it has only invested about $20 million. It would seem that its governance leaves a lot to be desired. In Africa, the national governments are beginning to get cold feet – your total investment only amounts to 5% of all direct foreign investment. For us in the West, all this makes us see your "New Silk Roads" as a "New Silk Rout"!

– I willingly admit that our plans for cooperation have not all been crowned with success but, as the old Russian adage goes – an adage frequently quoted by comrade Vladimir Putin during our meetings in the Kremlin: "He who takes no risks, drinks no champagne"! As for Italy, there's no need to worry on our account. We didn't buy the port of Trieste, simply because we already own on average 10% of all European ports. For us, first and foremost, it's all about managing the bottleneck that has a crucial effect on your imports, since almost 90% of the world's freight traffic is still by sea. Secondly, it's about taking our revenge on history: in the 20th century, we had to agree to "unfair" concessions for Hong Kong, Canton and Shanghai; in the 21st century, we shall control access to Europe. Once again, our inspiration has come from one of your own great men: Bill Gates. In the late 1990s, he said, with regard to the technology bubble, "We always overestimate the change that will occur in the next two years and underestimate the change that will occur in the next ten." This bodes well for our "New Silk Roads": they started out as an economic program, but, over time, their achievement will be geopolitical. Your problem is that you are too impatient! What's more, the American investment guru, Warren Buffet, agreed with me when he commented on the short-termism of your reasoning when applied to the US financial markets: "The stock exchange is a device for transferring wealth from the impatient to the patient." Time is on our side, all the more so since no country any longer considers the USA to be a trustworthy ally.

The great American denial

– There I have to agree with you, and it's a real problem for my country. We are well aware that the USA has successively betrayed Egypt, Saudi Arabia and the Kurds. The next victims risk being the Israelis – hence their recent improbable *rapprochement* with Saudi Arabia to face up to Iran. The day will come when the USA finally realizes that Iran – with a population of 80 million, including one of the world's largest proportions of highly-educated young people – is one of the most promising pockets of growth in the world. Donald Rumsfeld, the former US Defense Secretary, said: "The mission determines the coalition." We now know that the USA will always follow the values of their interests rather than the interests of their values. The French gave the East Coast the Statue of Liberty; it's a shame that our friends in Singapore have omitted to give the West Coast the Statue of Responsibility.

– Lord Fitzbacon, you have to admit that the world is changing. I would rather quote our mutual friend, Henry Kissinger, who said during a "Lunch with the FT": "I think Trump may be one of those figures in history who appears from time to time to mark the end of an era and to force it to give up its old pretenses." But you refuse to listen to him; you still think Trump was a temporary aberration for American democracy, whereas we have realized that he heralded the post-industrial decline of the (Dis-)United States.

– Don't underestimate Uncle Sam! There are still a lot of good things left.

– There's no danger of that. We never forget what it says in *The Art of War*: "Invincibility depends on oneself; the enemy's vulnerability on him." No, what we liked about Trump – and I would never admit this in public – is that Trump is Chinese, and this made negotiations so much easier.

– What do you mean, "Trump is Chinese"?

– He has all the main character traits. First of all, he is a real estate "crook" – a type we know only too well in China. Secondly, he tore up treaties that tied the hands of the USA – the COP21, the Trans-Pacific Partnership, the de-nuclearization agreement with Iran –, which provoked less of an uproar from my compatriots than from yours. Thirdly, whenever we talked business, he would say, "See with Jared for the practical details." Like him, we are not averse to mixing business and family business. So, you will understand that, when I landed at Mar-a-Lago in Florida to visit my friend Donald, I didn't feel as if I was playing an away game; I felt at home, even if each goal scored double points! Another thing: remember that Donald Trump barked a lot but didn't bite very often.

– That's why it's almost certainly in your interest not to move too much – like the goalkeeper when there's a penalty kick. The problem for the West is that it's us that the USA is attacking, by taxing European products. Since the

2008 financial crisis, $350 billion of fines have been inflicted on the world banking system. Only a part of these has been paid by American banks; the rest has been paid by European banks – who have now been relegated to League Division II. To American eyes, Europe has lost its strategic value ever since the collapse of the USSR. As the German Chancellor Angela Merkel said recently in public, we have to learn to live without America. But for us in Britain, the problem is that this would be a complete U-turn, bearing in mind the past. This is why all our hopes are pinned on a Democratic administration that will make it possible to re-establish our historical links.

– Personally, I don't believe in the Democratic lifebelt. President Biden is going to give you "Obama, Season 3". I don't want this to be a spoiler for the series, but I think we are about to see a major disruption in American history, a real tidal wave.

– And where is this tidal wave supposed to come from?

– As always, it's a question of demographics – an issue that is all too often ignored. A country's demographic is all-important; it's a supertanker that takes fifteen years to change course. Today, the white 60% of the population dominate the 40% who are ethnic minorities: about 19% are Hispanic, 15% are Afro-American, 5% are Asian, and 1% are Native Americans; minorities whose exceptional assimilation into the melting pot led to American hegemony in the 20th century. US birth figures suggest that by 2035 – in only 15 years time – for the first time, white people will have lost control of their country. This is producing real paranoia, for they feel threatened by an internal ethnic menace that will dictate American policy in the future, including foreign affairs. Any threat to American interests abroad will be seen as secondary. Hence the US withdrawal from its sphere of influence; yesterday in Europe, today in the Middle East, tomorrow supposedly in Asia. Remember that President Obama already announced a future swing in American foreign policy from the Middle East to Asia, even though 80% of his troops were still stationed in the Middle East.

– Well, at least that would have the advantage of preventing a Third World War…

– In fact, what we should be thinking about is peace, not war.

The Sino-American "Cold Peace"

– That's always best. Churchill is supposed to have said that wars were like love affairs: "Easy to declare, always painful to end." But knowing how to keep the peace is quite another matter.

"War impossible, peace improbable"

– We are in a situation that's completely the reverse of that of the post-war years. In 1947, Raymond Aron summed up the Cold War as follows: "Peace impossible, war improbable." Today, it's the opposite: war with the USA is impossible, for our economies are too intertwined, which was not the case with the USSR. And peace is improbable, for the USA is accusing us of stealing their technology and we are accusing them of stealing our development. So we're in for a few decades of "Cold Peace", for which we are going to have to invent a *modus operandi.*

– So, for you, there is no "Thucydides trap" that Graham Allison described so well in his remarkable book *Destined for War.*

– One can never be sure of anything, and, for several years now, it's become obvious that war is "paying off " again. Although American intervention in Iraq and Afghanistan ended disastrously and cost the tidy sum of $2,000 billion over more than ten years –10% of which went on air conditioning for the GIs! –, since Vladimir Putin's military intervention in Georgia, force seems to "pay off". That's the message that Turkey wants to get over with regard to Syria and Libya.

– But doesn't the real art of war consist in not making war?

– Of course it does. Even more so when, from a military standpoint – and this must not go any farther than this room – we are still lagging far behind the USA. It spends $600 billion every year on defense, whereas we only spend $200 billion, external defense and internal security combined. We have taken lessons from past conflicts between rising powers and established powers, and the way in which these conflicts were defused. For example, there was the conflict between Spain and Portugal in the 16th century that was quelled by papal intervention. Problems between the USA and the UK at the turn of the 20th century didn't reach the conflict stage because, just in time, both protagonists recognized their relative weakness and the bonds of a common culture. The antagonism between the USA and the USSR didn't lead to direct warfare because the Americans had the patience to wait for the outcome of the Soviet Union's decline. And, as a final example, the rivalry between a reunified Germany, France and the UK in 1990 was strangled at birth by multilateral institutions.

– Yes, papal intervention may have worked in the 16th century, but I can hardly see you being daunted by any armored divisions sent by Pope Francis! The other examples wouldn't work either as you are too proud of your cultural uniqueness, you don't care a fig for multilateral bodies, and, as far as the decline of the USA is concerned, let's hope you will have the patience to wait for the outcome and that the USA will come to a peaceful recognition of its relative decline.

– You will observe that the Covid-19 pandemic in the first quarter of 2020 was the first promising sign of that. It showed up some striking shortcomings in the American public health system, whereas we were going full speed in copying the Korean 3T strategy: Testing, Tracking, Treating – which proved highly successful.

– Yes, but don't forget that the USA saw Covid-19 as a sort of Pearl Harbor attack, for which you should expect them to take their revenge one day. We must do everything possible to prevent this revenge from reaching anything as horrific as Hiroshima or Nagasaki.

– And that's why, at the outset, our "Cold Peace" will take the form of a technological war.

Tech war, not trade war

– But it looks much more like a trade war.

– No, that was how President Trump wanted to see it. Following his own advice in *The Art of the Deal*, he pretended to want one thing to give him a better negotiating position for the thing that really interested him. A trade war is not the issue. Don't you think it paradoxical that the US – a superpower – would be fighting to export agricultural produce, whilst China – a rising power – was seeking to export high-tech products? What's more, let me remind you that sales by American companies implanted in China amount to almost $200 billion and this, combined with American exports to China, makes for much more balanced exchanges between the two countries. For instance, Apple alone sells almost $45 billion worth of goods in China every year. You can add to this about $50 billion reaped by the quartet of Qualcomm, Intel, Broadcom and Micron. Furthermore, out of the 25 companies in China who export the most to the USA, only five are Chinese groups: 14 are Taiwanese, four are American, two are Korean, and one is from Hong Kong. Let me end by reminding you that our exports, net of all imports, only account for 2% of our GDP and have hardly contributed at all to our growth for several years now. So, for us, this is not the real issue.

– What is the real issue then?

– The technology war, of course! What triggered it was the attempt by the "Chinese" Broadcom company to take over the American Qualcomm company for $117 billion. President Trump put a stop to it in March 2018. And yet, we didn't put a foot wrong: we proposed to move Broadcom's head office to the USA and showed that the company had its roots in Singapore. But friend Donald Trump couldn't stomach the fact that an Asian group was capable of shelling out over $100 billion to acquire a technological nugget – and, what's more, an American nugget! Up to then, it had been the prerogative of American giants to amass such a colossal financial strike force. So, he took the key decision to put a spanner in the works of our technological upgrading.

– Hence the focus on Huawei...

– In fact, he started with ZTE. The USA suddenly halted the supply of American components to ZTE in the spring of 2018. Since then, we have been obliged to give American auditors access to ZTE's offices at any moment, supposedly to verify that it is not trading with Iran. Of course, we're not taken in by this. This "one-sided treaty" is the modern version of a concession, and is totally unacceptable in the long term.

– And yet, the Huawei group seems to be on the way to getting similar treatment.

– Yes, but with a few changes in the timescale. We've managed to make our American counterparts understand – but for how long, I don't know – that, in the field of semi-conductors, Huawei is the equivalent of Lehmann Brothers in the the field of investment banking, and that to knock down one of the pillars of an industry that is a sort of ecosystem would have global consequences. For the moment, they've agreed to spread their retaliatory measures over time, but this doesn't change anything for us. We now know that we have to build a new ecosystem that is totally independent of the USA.

– But what strikes me is that Huawei and ZTE are the only two representatives of China that seem to have overtaken their American counterparts in terms of pure technological development. In one sense, I wonder if what you regard as a success isn't more a question of a strategic decision on the part of the Americans. About 20 years ago, America chose to count on the prospect of value creation in telecommunications moving to applications – like Google and Facebook – and to cellphones – like those produced by Apple. On the other hand, network manufacturers like Nokia and Ericsson in Europe and Cisco in the USA saw their value stagnate – at best. This choice proved to be judicious until the arrival of 5G, a technology aimed more at B2B than B2C – companies rather than consumers. 5G shifts part of the intelligence of a network to "the edge", as specialists call it. That's why I believe that the current US strategy is an attempt to stop the spread of 5G throughout the world for four to five years, so as to give the American telecommunications industry time to catch up. And I ask myself whether or not you'll be able to keep your own technological lead when you're up against the USA's response capability.

– It's nice of you to have pointed out the mistakes the USA has made because of its arrogance. Today, China produces 90% of the world's IT hardware; the West has left us control of its manufacture. This will be an enormous asset to us in any future trade negotiations, since the world has no credible alternative to China for supplying these goods in the short term. Another lever – more difficult to admit publicly – is the knowledge we have acquired about cybersecurity. If the need arises, we can use this in an offensive – rather than defensive – move, backed up by our space and satellite technology. So, you can be assured that we shall be able to defend ourselves perfectly well in this technology war. Perhaps we should take our inspiration from Czar Alexander III of Russia and his famous motto, "Russia has only two allies: the Army and the Navy." We know this only too well, including with regard to Taiwan.

– You do realize, don't you, that, for the Americans, Taiwan is the red line not to be crossed?

– Taiwan is a purely internal matter for China; it is no business of the Americans nor of anyone else except the Chinese. We have always said that reunification would take place some time during the 21st century. Little do they realize it, but it is the Americans themselves who are speeding things up. At present, they are banning Taiwanese semi-conductor factories from delivering to Chinese customers, and this leaves us no choice but to bring Taiwan into our own ecosystem as quickly as possible. What we used to consider simply as a new geostrategic direction taken by history, has now become an urgent economic necessity.

– But the case of Taiwan is very different from that of Hong Kong, because its population is already used to democracy, its institutions are stable and its technological lead over the rest of the world was shown again recently during the tsunami of the summer of 2020. The American company Intel publicly admitted that it is lagging behind TSMC, the Taiwanese company to which it subcontracted the manufacture of five-nanometer semi-conductors. And it's not just a question of economics and technology. If I organized a debate in the House of Lords and invited one of your diplomats as well as a representative from Taiwan, I would bet that your envoy would leave the chamber for fear of losing face when ideas were exchanged during the debate. You have to admit that the Taiwanese have built one of the most sophisticated cultures in the world, based on the best elements of your civilization and half a century of Japanese occupation. Starting with their cuisine!

– That's why we are delighted that 40% of their exports are to Mainland China today. We were enthusiastic when Terry Gou, who founded the Foxconn Group, stood in the last presidential elections in Taiwan which, unfortunately, didn't produce the expected result. Given the pressure from the Americans, we simply can't wait indefinitely. We know full well that this is a marathon enterprise, that it will be won in the first stages of the race, and that this will necessitate the best possible organization of our resources, to be put to full use later on. Comrade Liu Mingfu, a military strategist and author of the essay *The Chinese Dream*, has summed it up perfectly: "The next three decades will be the period when competition between the USA and China will be fiercest.

In the first decade, we shall catch it up; in the second, we shall be running neck and neck; and in the third, we shall overtake it."

– So the European Commission was right when, in March 2019, it redefined your country as "an economic competitor in the pursuit of technological leadership and a systemic rival promoting alternative models of governance."

Eurasia Felix?

– I deeply regret that Europe seems to be aligning itself blindly with the American position. This relinquishing of your independence – should it be confirmed – would lead you to become more and more a vassal of America.

The systemic rival

– When you came to power in 2012, we thought a *rapprochement* between our two systems might be in the offing but, you must admit, this hasn't happened. We had thought you were open to further economic reforms and yet, since 2015, you've sought to give preference to SOE – state-owned enterprises. From a multilateral standpoint, whether it be the World Health Organization, Interpol or the Asian Infrastructure Investment Bank, you have first and foremost tried to impose your standards, disregarding international requirements. The case of Interpol illustrates this particularly well because you arrested its president, Meng Hongwei – whom you yourself had appointed – in China. This grotesque situation caused the French cartoonist Plantu to draw one of his best cartoons for *Le Monde*: it showed an elderly Chinese woman in a French police station, telling them that her husband had gone missing, and a policeman telling her: "Ask Interpol!" Even when it comes to the environment, after a harmonization of interests at COP21, you nevertheless decided to go your own way in 2019 and considerably reduced your investments. You promote a system that, above all, seeks to protect its "Chinese features" and to use them to your advantage.

– My dear Lord Fitzbacon, if you are honest with yourself, you will realize that, since I came to power, I have reformed China more and faster than anyone before me. When I launched the anti-corruption campaign in 2012, no one believed in my determination, notably your Western press. You can see how much more efficient our Communist Party has become today, and this means we won't share the fate of our late Soviet cousin. As for economic organization, our domestic "financial crisis" of 2015, marked by an extremely volatile Chinese stock exchange during that summer, forced us to control market forces in order to avoid the crises you have found yourself up against in the West. Our Central Bank intervened directly at the beginning of August 2015 to burst the speculation bubble when valuations had reached three times their book value, which we deemed unrealistic. In your part of the world, no regulator has had the courage to intervene in such a preventative way. So, for us, reform never means freeing the markets, because we believe that it is the government's duty to maintain social harmony rather than let bubbles form and explode for the benefit of a few speculators.

– In the West we see this above all as a negation of the market economy. What's more, the European Commission has refused to grant you a market economy status within the framework of the World Trade Organization. You're still protecting your market rather than reforming your inefficient state sector. In this, you seem to be denying the legacy of Deng Xiaoping and returning to that of Mao.

– My dear sir, you are right – the "Deng Xiaoping era" is now behind us; there is no question of keeping a low profile any longer.

– That's exactly what Britons like me are afraid of, and I would add that, as a European, I have always been violently opposed to Brexit and remain deeply attached to Europe. I fear a "Yemenization of Europe" where China and the USA will fight their battles, not on their own soil, but on neutral ground, just like Iran and Saudi Arabia who are tackling each other in Yemen. If Europe doesn't get its act together, it will end up having its trade taxed by the USA and its technology pillaged by your cyber-attacks. Those are humiliations that we are not prepared to accept. Under pressure from you, HSBC bank, historically the most influential European institution in the world, recently had to ask its CEO, John Flint, to step down after only 18 months in office. Your words remind me of Theresa May's visit to Beijing, during which journalists wondered what would be on the menu for the state banquet; one of them suggested, "The United Kingdom"!

– Please, that's enough about the UK of the past. We have to concern ourselves with the world of tomorrow.

"G minus 2": towards a new inclusive leadership

– Then take heed of something said by James Bullard, the President of the Federal Reserve Bank of Saint Louis: "Let's stop believing the world will be normal next year!"

– First of all, you must accept that the West is disappearing; it's what you are now calling "Westlessness" in English. One could already see this in the summer of 2019 when, because of so much disagreement, the G7 ended without any joint communiqué. In actual fact, the term "Westlessness" takes its inspiration from the work of my friend Yan Xueitong, head of the International Relations Institute at Tsinghua University. For him, "chaos and disorder are becoming the normal status of the world. International standards will no longer be dictated by Western liberalism. In the absence of dominant values, competing strategies that respect neither standards nor commitments will prevail during a transition period in which economic sanctions and protectionism will serve to establish each country's position in terms of power. China's position will be greatly strengthened by the divisions in the West."

– That's exactly why it's extremely urgent to rethink world governance. The crisis we have just been through is totally different from the one in 2008. During that one, it has to be said that it was thanks to the visionary mind of the French President, Nicolas Sarkozy – even if, being British, I would never admit it publicly – that world governance grew in stature. The G7 extended itself to a G20 which was a far better representation of the world's economic balance of power. In 2020, the opposite was true, for the crying lack of international cooperation during the crisis saw the G20 shrink to a G2 – China and the USA – and now this has even been reduced to a "G zero".

– The world has simply become bipolar.

– No, it hasn't. And that's the whole problem. The USA's soft power was wiped out by President Trump, because the rest of the Western camp no longer saw Uncle Donald as the protector of its values. As for sharp power, that doesn't work any more either given the extent of the present crisis, which demands a global response. The best illustration of this is the situation of OPEC in the oil sector. Put Russia, Saudi Arabia and Texas in the same room –three powers, all of them with a taste for sharp power – and you will end up with a barrel of crude priced at $20! The former CEO and chairman of Schlumberger said to the *Financial Times*, "OPEC, as the so-called central bank of oil, has disappeared!", because the fall in demand linked to the crisis is such that the solution can only come from a new holistic approach.

– And, to your way of thinking, what would this new approach be?

– "G minus 2"!

– What do you mean by "G minus 2"?

– "G minus 2" would be an inclusive global governance bringing the whole world together with the exception of the USA and China. Remember what Henry Kissinger said about the Iran-Iraq conflict: "It's a pity both sides can't lose." That's exactly what the rest of the world will hope for, if you and America don't stop being so childish.

– That's totally unrealistic! I think your "G minus 2" will come to the same sticky end as Goldman Sachs' "BRICS" – a ridiculous concept that only served to enrich the bank. What do we have in common with Brazil or South Africa, not to mention India?

– I am glad that my words shock you, for this just strengthens my belief in the idea, which I originally got from India, Japan and Australia, who managed to anticipate the current situation. Rather than adopt the bureaucratic and inefficient idea of a customs, economic and monetary union between them, like the one in Europe, they opted for an *ad hoc* alliance based on specific issues where their interests came into line – interests that generally go against yours. The idea would be to extend this approach to the rest of the world. Take the example of Iran, where the blackmail and extra-territoriality practiced by the Americans are quite simply unacceptable.

– Ah which gave us the magnificent opportunity to sign an energy supply contract with Iran worth over $400 billion

– Whereas we, in Europe, bowed and scraped before Washington. When the Total Group had to leave Iran, President Macron simply said, "I am not the President of Total,". In order to trade with Iran, we are not only going to have to ally ourselves with our European neighbors, but also with Russia, by means of a currency basket that excludes the dollar. Similarly, Europe has to reinvent Willy Brandt's *Ostpolitik* and bring Europe together again, even including Russia – the "poor power" that could easily be reminded that, in just one year, your GDP has grown by the equivalent of theirs. This is why it's going to be difficult for Russia to hope that it will one day sign a win-win agreement with you, even given President Putin's brilliant negotiating skills. Similarly, we shall take great pleasure in refreshing the memories of our East European friends, who seem to be showing the first symptoms of Alzheimer's and have forgotten that, from 2000 to 2017, your total direct investment in their region came to only $6.3 billion as compared to $140 billion from Western Europe.

– Well, good luck with your "G minus 2", but I'm afraid you're not going to get any further than the countries that have been non-aligned since the 1950s. You would save yourself some time if you realized that all your post-war international organizations created under American influence – NATO, the UN, etc. – are now brain dead.

– That's why this "G minus 2" stage will only last for a short time. Once a new global governance has been well established, we shall invite the two major powers to join us. Our ultimate aim must be to build the *Eurasia Felix* that is so needed by the 21st century. The 20th century was centered on the *rapprochement* between Europe and the USA; China's mission in the 21st century is to build a bridge between China and Europe.

Avoiding "social distancing' between China and Europe

– But that's exactly what we're doing with our proposals for "win-win" cooperation with you. For instance, in December 2020, we signed the Comprehensive Agreement on Investment with Brussels – a historical step, after seven years of negotiations. According to Rhodium's experts, by the end of 2020, Chinese investment in Europe – excluding the UK – totaled only $140 billion, whilst European investment in China – excluding British investment – only totaled $180 billion, which is marginal considering our respective GDPs. We are opening up new sectors to European investment, such as financial and healthcare services, the cloud, and electric vehicles…

– …whilst, at the same time, you have been asking your Education Minister to close down cooperation between China and foreign countries in the field of higher education – 20% of it went in 2018 and, now, almost all of it.

– Our Education Minister doesn't need any lectures from abroad, and certainly not from his British counterpart. Your last minister, Jo Johnson, "Bojo's" own brother, chose to resign so as to spend *less* time with his family – that must be a first!

– But exchanges between universities were one of the very things that made the USA strong in the 20th century. No, the answer must come from Europe, not from you, and we have to copy you. Today, you have a competitive advantage over us of 100 to 1, and we must make inroads into this. It's not a question of reducing our trade deficit, but of reducing our knowledge deficit. Only 600,000 Westerns live on Mainland China, whereas your diaspora comprises 70 million Chinese who have adopted Western manners. In our systemic rivalry, you master both systems, whilst we don't understand yours. So, we have to study how you function so that we can get a better idea of your strengths and weaknesses. During the last two crises, your strength has dazzled and surprised us. We now have to work on discerning your weaknesses – that's the only self-protection that will be effective if we want to do some straight talking during any future negotiations.

– I'm curious to know what you think these weaknesses are.

– We're still working on this in the House of Lords, but certain avenues are emerging. Your main strength lies in your ability to federate 1.4 billion Chinese, whilst our attempts to bring together 400 million Europeans have failed lamentably. As for your weaknesses, I would differentiate between the short term – which is our main priority – and the long term. Today, your short-term weakness is the prevailing uncertainty about the recovery of consumer demand, which has driven the economy over the last ten years. Your consumers are afraid of inflation, particularly in the food sector, given the recent pork crisis. They have considerable debts, but their salaries remain at a standstill or are even falling. They are still worried that the Covid-19 virus will return, and they know that, if it does, they will be the last to know. Regarding investment, the treasuries of small- and medium-sized companies have been drained, in a country where it is common practice to wait nine months before being paid. And yet almost all job creation comes from these

SMEs. Bank loans – essentially from state banks – have always been looked on with mistrust since the second half of 2018, even more so since there is the specter of a margin call on loans, which made it possible for your state banks to take control of several private companies in the second quarter of 2018. This has left indelible traces. But, personally, I have great confidence in your country's surprising ability to bounce back. What interests me more are your long term structural weaknesses.

– Are you sure you're not confusing us with the West?

– No, you have some Achilles heels. First of all, there is your financial system – no country has ever become a great power without a solid financial system. Your four main state banks – the Bank of China, the Industrial and Commercial Bank of China, the China Construction Bank and the Agricultural Bank of China – are the subject of an aphorism that is going round the City of London: "When it comes to Chinese banks, there is nothing right on the left of the balance sheet, so there is nothing left on the right of the balance sheet." The S&P Global Rating agency estimates that, today, these four banks need to recapitalize to the tune of $220 billion, to conform to international capitalization standards that will apply to them in 2025.

– We already recapitalized the Agricultural Bank of China in 2018 at $15 billion, by issuing the largest private investment operation ever carried out in our A-shares market. So we are fully equipped to meet anything our banking system may need.

– That's excellent news, since 20% of it is still in the hands of ineffectual regional banks, a fact which caused the former governor of the Chinese central bank to say, on leaving his post in 2018, "My successor will have to face a 'Minsky' moment". He was referring to the economist Hyman Minsky, an expert on financial crises. And I won't go into the question of your shadow financing, especially "shadow lending", which reached the astronomical level of $190 billion before your regulator intervened to limit losses, which today are estimated at over $100 billion. According to Morgan Stanley, you are going to need on an annual basis between $100 billion and $200 billion of foreign capital over the next decade. What's more, your banking industry must be in a disastrous state for your friends at the HNA holding company to have any interest whatsoever in taking a 10% share in Deutsche Bank – probably the most derided bank in Europe: In 2018, it still had 643 staff members whose ridiculously high salaries made them millionaires every year, whilst its stock market value continued to plummet! It's hardly surprising that, in the end, Wang Jian, the co-founder of HNA, finally wanted to step back from the move… Unfortunately, the poor man took a literal step back that led to his demise when he was in Bonnieux, in Provence: he mounted a low wall overlooking a sheer drop to take a selfie, and fell 15 meters to his death.

– Lord Fitzbacon, you seem to be forgetting that four ingredients are necessary for there to be any banking crisis, and, fortunately, there are only three in our case: there is the leverage effect of indebtedness, lack of transparency and credit risk – all of which are present, I grant you. But the fourth – lack of liquidity – is something we still control in the best possible way – enough to confound all the prophets of doom over the last decades. I might also attempt to reassure you by saying that our real estate is no more over-valued than the US S&P stock market index.

– Another weakness is your inability to adapt to local conditions when you "play away". Despite fears of a "Chinese invasion", your investments, particularly in Europe, are, as you have pointed out, very modest. Germany has invested at least six to eight times as much in China as you have in return, and France has invested three times as much. What's more, not all your investments have met with success – far from it. Look at the astronomical sums you have had to pay up front to acquire capital in Kuka, to pay for Geely's share in Daimler, to enable your CIC sovereign fund to get a share in Eutelstat, to buy Club Méditerranée, Syngenta, Dufry, Thomas Cook and Sonia Rykiel... We Europeans also know how to make "win-win" deals, but deals in our favor! And look at what happened when the Hong Kong Stock Exchange proposed buying the London Stock Exchange: the LSE Board of Directors refused to see your Hong Kong friends – they didn't even offer them a cup of tea! But your worst mishap has been the US Treasury bill affair: you still have $1,000 billion dollars invested in them and what returns will you get back? Peanuts – at best. You are still prisoners of the dollar, which continues to finance two-thirds of world trade whilst American exports only account for 10% of global exports. Now there's a topic where any collaboration would be in our mutual interest.

– Believe me, as far as currency is concerned, time is on our side. When you landed in Beijing, you can't have failed to notice that our RMB currency has doubled its value in 10 years against your pound sterling. So, we will have great pleasure in returning to London to "do the sales" which might include the Crown Jewels one day – that is, if they haven't already been put up for sale on WeChat by Prince Harry!

– I agree that time is undoubtedly on your side when it comes to the dollar but, when it comes to your relations with the rest of the world, I'm not so sure. In the second decade of this century, you accounted for half of all growth worldwide; in 2019 it was only a third – as compared to 30% for the rest of Asia, 11% for the USA and 4% for Europe – and, in 2040, you will only account for a quarter of it. The main argument you use in power politics – your economic importance relative to other countries – is tending to wear away. What's more, I can see an awakening in Europe, under the twin leadership of Ms von der Leyen and Chancellor Angela Merkel, during the current discussions following on from the Comprehensive Agreement on Investment. There is now a pan-European approach based on a far more substantial qualitative screening, and on much greater co-operation with other Asian countries. You'll see that, with the new Commission, Europe will at last be able to put its house in order. This might even be the best surprise in store in this post-Covid 19 era. The world will discover that nine of the 19 countries in the euro zone have balanced budgets. Because of the Bundesbank's unfortunate outlay on Spain and Italy –the extravagant sum of around one trillion euros – through the "Target 2" system, Germans have had to face up to the painful alternative of "double or quits". As good Europeans, they have decided to double, notably by agreeing to the €750 billion European recovery fund, but this time with the express condition that they should be the ones who are really in charge of Europe.

– I must say that we're extremely hopeful that our relationship with Ms von der Leyen will be a fruitful one. But if Europe's only aim is to introduce a new form of protectionism, this will lead to the same debacle as the USA has suffered in the steel sector.

– That's interesting advice coming from you, an expert on protectionism! But, don't worry, we're fully aware that the dangers of de-globalization could be worse than those of globalization. On the contrary, I think we shall succeed if we apply the principles of António Gutteres, the current UN Secretary General, that he mentioned during his "Lunch with the FT". He said that any negotiation between two people begins with six discussion partners. All of them are not just themselves, but also what they believe themselves to be, as well as what the people opposite believe them to be. Guterres explained that, as an arbitrator of negotiations, he has spent his life bringing the number of negotiators down from six to two – which is their real number. If the British and the Europeans want to build a "*Eurasia Felix*", we have not only to understand you better, but also to solve our own internal identity crisis, get rid of our arrogance, and no longer worry about hiding our weaknesses. When talking about Europe, the former Prime Minister of Italy, my friend Enrico Letta, asked the question: "How can we go from strength based on our economic strength to strength based on our attractiveness and the influence of our values?" For instance, how should we approach climate change and social responsibility – issues that our countries will come together on well before the USA? The new "Eurasia" of the 21st century will demand a multicultural approach, in complete contrast to the American cultural hegemony of the 20th century.

– I like your idea of a "Eurasia" that will stretch from our frontiers right up to Europe. I will bear that in mind. Only our two ancient civilizations, because of their complexity and contradictions, will have the flexibility to build it. I shall have to see how we can develop this concept, without sacrificing our "Chinese characteristics". Perhaps I shall call it "EuraXia".

– President Xi, I can't promise you any engagement on my part unless you stop trying systematically to gain the advantage. I expect that, in the meantime, our countries will go through an intermediate phase during which we shall swing between cooperation, competition and confrontation. To my mind, if you play the game, it is cooperation that will prevail over time.

– I can't think of any better prospect with which to end our discussion. I believe we've agreed to disagree on a large number of points, but I accept what you believe to be my mission in the 21st century. As a token of my gratitude, I have a very special mission for you: please take this precious gift back to Her Majesty Queen Elizabeth. It is the pistol that Queen Victoria gave to our emperor just before the opium wars. If we manage to build a "EuroXia", I'm sure we won't be needing it in our future relationship.

5

Thursday – Shenzhen, on the Huawei campus, Dr von Sprungdurch-Technik

> *"Performance is the only protection."*
> Carlos Tavares, CEO of Stellantis

– Doctor von Sprungdurch-Technik, it is a great pleasure to see you again here in Shenzhen, on the campus of my friend Ren Zhengfei. I hope you noticed the black swans by the lake. They are symbolic of "non-complacency within the corporate culture" and are Ren's way of reminding visitors that the Huawei Group is ready to adapt to any eventual change in the business climate – probably the right philosophy for our interview. The last time I had the pleasure of seeing you was during one of Chancellor Angela Merkel's annual visits to China. I have a great deal of respect for your country, which provides us with 40% of all our imports from Europe, and I share Henry Kissinger's regret that your nation is "too big for Europe, too small for the world." So, today, I am delighted to be able to listen to the views of one of the German industrialists who has had the most success in China.

– President Xi, this is a great honor for me. The group I inherited from my father is now a multinational with branches in 93 countries, but I have to say that, although yours may be one of the most fascinating and stimulating countries to get to know, trying to gain a foothold here is an extremely grueling experience. Competition here is fiercer than anywhere else, fanned by what I would call an insatiable appetite.

An obsession with growth

– If you were in my shoes, how would you analyze China's growth prospects?

– I think it's the same for countries as it is for businesses: we are all subject to economic cycles that we have to adapt to. Today, I think you are bringing one cycle to a close and opening another. Since the Great Financial Crisis of 2008, your growth has been driven by three factors that are now slowing down.

The three setbacks to Chinese growth

– But, believe me, our economy is not stagnating.

– No, but you must evolve, so as to satisfy your people's obsession with growth. For the last ten years, your growth has primarily been based – artificially – on rampant indebtedness, the rise of which has been twice as fast in China as in the West. This has had the mechanical effect of benefiting the real estate market, which seems to have peaked in 2017 when new building totaled 1.4 billion square meters, with 25% of funding coming from state subsidies in one form or another. This has had a harmful effect in that 30% of families now own at least one vacant apartment where their one and only child can live in the future. It has also had another – disastrous – effect for, in your largest cities – the Tier 1 category –, it will take a property owner an average of 40 years to pay back a mortgage, whereas your buildings only have an average 30-year lifespan. The same goes for the market in office space. According to Savills, who are experts in the field, 22% of office space is vacant in Shenzhen, and almost 40% in Zhuhai and Foshan in the Guangdong region. What's more, a unique feature of your financial system is that it makes de-leveraging ineffective since it uses up bank capital instead of freeing it up. Junk assets that don't appear on the balance sheet are re-integrated into the balance sheets of financial institutions, and this is one of the reasons why, every time you've tried to restrain the growth of your total social funding, the economy has been in danger of collapsing, as in the second quarter of 2018, and you've had to reprime the pump.

– You forget to mention that our banks are only too happy to repossess real estate that has provided security for loans, and whose intervening price rise more than covers the initial outlay.

– The second growth factor has become the source of a slow-down: access to American technology. Ever since President Trump, an increasingly strict embargo has been placed upon it. When it comes to technology, we're seeing the coming of a bipolar world that will probably reorganize itself after a transition period. The third growth factor has become a brake: the incredible market penetration of the smartphone. It has been the first truly global success in the history of electronic consumer goods with sales reaching a peak in 2018 and then, for the first time, decreasing. This initially meant that your local manufacturers – Huawei, Vivo and Oppo – increased their market share. But now, even they are going to have to content themselves with merely a replacement market. So, there have been three winds which blew in your favor in the past, but are now blowing in the opposite direction. This is why Michael Pettis – an expert in the field and a professor at Peking University – has said that, if you exclude your over-investment, swollen by over-indebtedness, your real growth rate is only 3%. Informed observers have remarked that your tax revenue in 2019 only increased by 3.8%, doubtless a good indicator of your real growth rate.

– Let me assure you, we are perfectly aware of the brakes you mention and have already been working for several years to re-balance our economy by increasing domestic consumption, which will have to drive the economy in the future. I spoke at length about this the day before yesterday with the eminent Italian sociologist Professor Leonarda da Vincierra from the University of Perugia, whom I'm sure you've met before.

– Yes, but domestic consumption will always compete with the need to save for a rainy day – given the lack of social infrastructure and the fact that bank deposits are not remunerated. You will be obliged to address the slow-down in the three factors I mentioned. Your people clearly expect to benefit from this growth, especially with regard to their purchasing power. It was a good move on your part to put off the arrival of a "prosperous China" until 2049, and to announce the more modest ambition of arriving at a "modern China" between 2020 and 2035. But when you're the head of a world-class company and have to present the annual accounts, I can guarantee that you're going to have big problems getting your shareholders to swallow a 15-year-long profit warning.

– On a more positive note, what do you see as the factors that will drive future growth?

"Qualitative" growth

– First of all, I think indebtedness has to be replaced by productivity, both of capital and of labor. Robert Kaplan, the highly-respected President and CEO of the Federal Reserve Bank of Dallas estimates that the potential growth rate of the USA will be limited to 1.5% in the future, because of its under-investment in education. Note that, in the USA, households only spend an average of 2% of their budget on higher education, as compared to as much as 15% in Asia. So, you should take any opportunity to speeding up your increases in productivity, especially since your population will age rapidly from 2020 onwards. Next, you will have to replace American technology by your own – technology that will be developed, I hope, with the help of European companies like mine. Lastly, the "B2C" internet of the smartphone must give up its seat to the "B2B" internet of the cloud – for companies – which will make it possible to digitize the whole of the economy and not only the sectors linked to consumption. In a word, I would say that your growth has to become "qualitative". What's more, a smaller yet more profitable growth rate is very good news for investors – it's always in the back of their minds that a third of the companies quoted on your local stock exchanges have never paid out dividends. Huang Guangyu, the former chairman of the GOME group, reminded us recently of past dangers. He was the richest man in China when he was sentenced to prison in 2008 and, when released in the summer of 2020, he observed that the Shanghai stock exchange index was at the same level as on the day he was arrested. With false innocence, he asked, "Has the market been closed for twelve years?"

– In what you say, the word that sticks out for me is productivity. We shall never be able to aspire to taking over world leadership from the USA if our productivity remains a third or a quarter of theirs. I have absolute confidence in the entrepreneurial ingenuity of my people. Look at Hong Kong where, at the height of the crisis in December 2019, the president of the Association of Public Toilets proposed to put out a call for tenders worldwide to develop urinals for women, so as to shorten waiting lines. He thought that there was potential in this for increasing productivity in offices!

– Hong Kong will always remain the same mega-city driven by its fascinating entrepreneurial energy – it has 1.6 million companies for 7 million inhabitants! The same impetus is coming out of Shenzhen, where 60% of the under-30s say they want to found their own company.

– However, I would add something to your concept of productivity – the environmental aspect, meaning a better use of natural resources, beginning with energy. We have just announced our aim of achieving carbon neutrality by 2060 with a peak in CO_2 emissions coming in 2030. We fully expect that the environmental quality of our economy will give us a competitive edge in the 21st century. In February 2021, China launched a carbon trading market, just like Europe, with the cost per ton quite low, at around $5. However, this should rise rapidly to become more punitive: $25 by 2030 and $100 by 2050. Experts at Goldman Sachs estimate that it will take a huge $400 billion of investment every year for 40 years in order to reach carbon neutrality in 2060. In 2020, we added almost 120 gigawatts to renewable energy sources – 70 gigawatts to wind turbines and 50 gigawatts to solar energy, which represent annual increases of 180% and 80% respectively. And the rest of the economy will have to follow. Some sectors, like the textile industry, will have to reform in any case because, as the second highest polluter in the world, it can't continue to have three-fifths of its production end up in the trash can or in the incinerator after 18 months. In the same way, the plastics industry will suffer from the revolution in packaging, which accounts for almost half of demand for its products. This will impact on the petrochemical sector, which consumes almost 15% of all oil extracted worldwide, and which will account for half of the growth in demand for oil between now and 2040. However, two-thirds of petrochemical production is linked to plastics, whose decline will be a saving grace. Hema, a distributor for Alibaba, has already come up with a most novel idea: anyone who comes to Hema to do their shopping and has a reusable shopping bag will be given green points; when enough points are accumulated, this will pay for a tree to be planted.

– You Chinese always have the ability to see things from a positive point of view.

– But, let's leave these few symbolic examples aside; the real answer to the question of our future growth will be in speeding up the adoption of technology.

"Tech it or leave it!"

– That was the whole basis for the United States' success throughout the 20th century.

– And it's what will decide who the winner will be in the 21st century and, in the case of technology, the winner takes all. Philippe Delmas, a former vice-president of Airbus, has observed that the "tech" revolution has turned a society based on exams into a society based on competitions, with winners and losers. Intel is still in control of 50% of microprocessor design after 50 years, Android and IoS now have 95% of the market in mobile operating systems, when they had only 5% in 2007. Half of all global internet traffic is in the hands of only four companies. Take the example of the top five companies on the S&P 500 stock exchange index in the years 2000 and 2020. Microsoft is the only one to have kept its place on the podium, whereas Cisco, Intel, General Electric and Walmart have been replaced by Apple, Amazon, Alphabet and Facebook. That sums up the effect of the digital tidal wave perfectly.

– I would add that the digital revolution doesn't only apply to companies, but to government organization as well. The two countries that have handled the Covid-19 crisis best – ahead of Germany – are Taiwan and South Korea, because of their 3Ts: Testing, Tracking and Treating. They used their technology resources to the best advantage, and you should take your lead from them.

– That's what we're doing with our major investment plan "New Infrastructures" to which we are going to devote $400 billion at the outset. We have seven clearly-defined priorities. Four of them are centered on the use of data: 5G networks, data centers, artificial intelligence, and the internet of industrial things. The other three are ultra-high voltage, Intercity trains and urban transit, and batteries for electric vehicles. May I remind you that we already invest almost $1,700 billion in infrastructure every year, whilst in the USA they are talking about an infrastructure recovery plan of $1,000 billion over 10 years. The wheel of history is turning! Do you remember that time when Tesla produced its quarterly results – supposedly record results as usual? It was the day when a large part of California was without electricity! Between now and 2050, our national leader in the field, the State Grid of China, wants to build a "web" of electricity, much like the web of the internet, that will enable us to use energy produced in Brazil while the Brazilians sleep.

– But aren't you worried that there will be a social crisis if these new technologies destroy too many jobs? It takes 10 workers to produce a diesel engine, three for a gasoline engine, and only one for an electric motor. It has been estimated that for every job Amazon creates, it destroys two.

– That's a complete red herring! In South Korea, for every 10,000 workers there are 530 robots, one of the highest rates in the world, and the unemployment rate is a mere 3.4%. Technology doesn't destroy jobs, it relocates them. I always like to quote the example of videoconferencing after the 9/11 attacks in 2001. Videoconferencing was supposed to reduce air traffic but, in fact, it helped it to grow back because people came together from the four corners of the earth for these conferences, which then made them want to meet each other in person.

– Let me come back to the "winner takes all" principle. I ask myself how you intend to catch up on the giant American companies that have got the lead over you. I don't suppose I need to remind you that Amazon's annual R&D budget is $30 billion and Microsoft's is $15 billion. If you add Google, Apple and Intel to that, you get a total of $75 billion – more than the R&D budget of France.

– But did you know that, today, half of the world's unicorns – companies valued at over $1 billion – are Chinese companies? Or that the Tencent Group has invested in over 800 companies, of which 160 are already unicorns? Or that it is about to invest $15 billion every year in artificial intelligence alone? If you add Baidu and the Ant group to Tencent, over half of all patents linked in blockchain are already Chinese. They are going to revolutionize supply chains, in combination with the drones produced by the market leader DJI, put into service with SF Express, our logistics giant.

– It's true to say that there are sectors today – like logistics and e-commerce – where starting from a blank page is an advantage, and this explains why long-established companies are having such trouble catching up.

– The long-established leaders that will lag farthest behind will be those that lack vision. And our vision for the next decade is clear: it's all about connectivity, which, in the future, will replace the smartphone as the main driving force for growth and which is a core factor in the concept behind our

Special Economic Zone of the Greater Bay Area in Guangdong. We intend to deploy this connectivity at three levels. First of all, connectivity between cities by means of high-speed Intercity trains. We invest $100 billion every year in our rail network, because the train is the most environmentally-friendly means of transport, and the one best suited to the sharing economy of the 21st century. It already takes 41% of passenger traffic, as compared to 27% who use the freeways. Secondly, connectivity within cities, so as to optimize the way population flow is handled, notably thanks to 5G – which we have been the first to use. 5G already has over 10 million subscribers, and Shanghai alone has already built 45,000 base stations whereas, in France, for example, the target is a mere 48,000 by 2025! Experts at China Mobile expect that the average subscriber will be accessing ten times as much data by 2025. The same reasoning is behind the fact that 60% of all optical fiber in the world is being laid in China. Thirdly, there is connectivity at human level – between you and connected objects – that will make it possible to develop digital services that will prevent us from falling into the middle income trap – a dangerous stage in a country's development. Our Greater Bay Area will be a concentrate of New York, San Francisco, Ohio and three of the largest ports in the world; in other words, an amazing mixture of finance, technology, manufacturing and logistics. Its development will be greatly helped by overseas Chinese, many of whom originally came from this region. It will develop a new Chinese lifestyle, just as the Beijing Olympics of 2008 marked the return of China to the world stage.

– I admire this vision you have of industry. It's a vision we are sadly lacking in Europe but, even so, I think you are underestimating the problems you're going to have carrying it out, because you've made three mistakes.

Three windows for Europe

– That's an interesting point of view. But are you sure you're not confusing us with the West? What are these so-called mistakes?

The loss of "our" United States

– They're three mistakes made at the same time and which are now putting you into a relatively weak position in the short term. First of all, you attacked the USA 10 years too soon. With regard to the 10 key industries that figure in your "Made in China 2025" plan, you are still far too dependent on American technology. By going completely against past practice and making it public that your ambition was to lead the world, the USA became aware of the threat you pose – a threat which it had not fully realized up to then. This has enabled it to put the brakes on your progress – for instance, in the fields of semi-conductors and operating systems. This has been particularly damaging because, before then, you couldn't have wished for a better USA: it was focused on the short term and agreed to transfer its technology in exchange for trade access to your market. It was very clever of you: you were getting the results of decades of research in exchange for a few years of sales revenue.

– You can't haven't read the McKinsey report. It pointed out that, today, Chinese imports of technology – IP and services combined – only account for 16% of our expenditure on R&D. Foreign companies already have 1,500 R&D centers in China. They are all working on "Made in China for China", pinpointing all of our own products and services that are neither suitable for the American market nor aim to be. What matters for our future is not American technology any more; it is our domestic demand.

Private! No entry!

– Maybe so. Now, you made your second mistake in the spring of 2018 when you broke the bond of trust between your government and the private sector, notably by limiting the bank loans the private sector could obtain to less than 20% of all loans granted in China – more than 80% going to the public sector. With the case of Huawei in point, it being the only Chinese technology company that has managed to destabilize the USA – and this is not just flattery because we are enjoying their hospitality today –, you concluded that companies working in close collaboration with the state – and under its influence – were the only ones capable of rivaling the West.

– If I were from Europe, I would share your fear of state intervention, for European governments are totally disconnected from the realities of industry – with the notable exception of your own country, Germany. And that's the reason why you are so successful in China. In 2019, a report – from McKinsey again – described how Chinese technological know-how fared on a global scale. It pointed out that our greatest successes were the result of coordination between the private sector and the state. The study analyzed our local and global market share as well as the efficiency of our local supply chain, and concluded that our manufacturers of solar panels were already world leaders in the field. It also said that the sectors in which China was highly likely to gain the upper hand were high-speed trains, digital payments, electric vehicles and wind turbines; the sectors where our potential leadership was limited by weaknesses in the local value chain included smartphones, cloud services and robotics; the areas in which we needed more time to become leaders were the aeronautical and semi-conductor industries. You can be sure that those are the areas in which we shall be redoubling our efforts in the coming years – and those highly-renowned consultancy firms of yours will be proved wrong.

– But you have to admit that state intervention can become nightmarish, for both your government and your private sector entrepreneurs. In 2019, you had to put a stop to subsidizing electric battery producers when subsidies had reached a grand total of almost $60 billion. It left you with just two "national champions", CATL and BYD. Yes, they supply two-thirds of your domestic market, but they are incapable of getting a foothold in other countries. LG Chemicals has 50% of the world market outside China, followed by its fellow-Korean Samsung with 20%, and the Japanese company Panasonic with 15%. In China, almost 500 companies that purported to be manufacturers of electric vehicles used these subsidies to speculate on the real estate market, on the pretext of building research centers. The city of Shenzhen spent almost $1 billion in subsidies and got only 16,000 electric buses in return – making the price of each bus somewhat expensive! You gave the FAW automobile group an insane credit line of 1,000 billion RMB – $150 billion! – to restructure the sector of your automobile industry that was failing. And, finally, in the field of semi-conductors, one of your "national champions", Tsinghua Unigroup, with links to the prestigious Tsinghua University, was in danger of defaulting on its loan of 64 billion RMB – almost $10 billion! It tried to transfer part of its assets to entities associated with Chongqing's municipal authority, after the authorities first in Shenzhen and then in Suzhou had declined the offer!

– Thank you Herr Doktor, for pointing out certain weaknesses in our system; I am endeavoring to correct them as the years go by. However, let me describe China in the words of someone who is a shrewd observer of this country, François Godement of the Institut Montaigne in Paris. I don't always agree with his analyses but I do agree when he said we are like a steam engine: there may well be a lot of wastage, but, in the end, we move forward.

The dreams and lies of Davos

– There remains the third mistake which, to my eyes, is the most incomprehensible. You seem to have gone back on all the promises you made in your historic speech at Davos in 2017. President Trump was offering you the chance to be part of a multilateralism that would enable you to reshuffle the world's pack of cards. It was offered to you on a plate, but instead you have preferred to intensify your bilateral attacks. First of all, you took against Canada after the arrest of Meng Wanzhou, the Finance Director of the Huawei Group. Then, against Sweden, which was getting too attached to human rights for your liking. After that, it was the United Kingdom, whose Prime Minister had criticized your actions in Hong Kong; then Vietnam, with a dispute over its territorial waters; then Australia, by taxing its exports. You have also come into conflict with African countries because of your mistreatment of their nationals in Guangdong. The list of your aggressive actions goes on and on, and the only result has been to strengthen anti-Chinese feeling throughout the world.

– That is a very one-sided way of putting it. May I point out that 40% of Chinese exports come from joint ventures with foreign companies. This so-called bilateralism, which you seem to be criticizing me for, is just as beneficial to you in our commercial dealings as it is for us.

– Don't get me wrong! There is nothing I want less than to end our mutually beneficial cooperation, like the cooperation my group has set up in your country. My concern is to avoid the cost that would be incurred by any future non-cooperation, notably if it were to concern our two countries. Look at what's happened to our French friends who, with their legendary arrogance, manage to cause grotesque situations like the one that involved the Wuhan P4 virology center. You Chinese took advantage of the petty squabbles between French Ministers and, in the end, gained control over a center entirely financed by France. But it was a Pyrrhic victory because the lab was useless when the Covid-19 virus made its appearance in Wuhan! Simply because the right training was never given, you didn't know how to use its ability to cope with circumstances involving extremely high-risks. It's as if I gave you the keys to my Ferrari without telling you that you had to take driving lessons in Maranello before being allowed to take the wheel.

– Please stop using the French example as a basis for making generalizations about how we should behave. You've known them long enough to know that they are a special case! Let me remind you that they are the ones who, for the trifling cost of €2.7 million a year, gave Shanghai access to 100 masterpieces from the Beaubourg museum's wonderful collection of modern art, second only in the world to the MoMA in New York. The Arab Emirates had to pay a billion in order to have a branch of the Louvre in Abu Dhabi.

– Once again, I have to admire your negotiating skills, but you must recognize that we need to change the way we think about relationships, and think about them in terms of continents if we want to ensure that they will be fruitful in the future. Do you see the value of the constructive criticism offered by my friend Joerg Wuttke, the President of the EU Chamber of Commerce in China?

Putting a stop to the "Yuan-way-street"

– Joerg is a good friend of China's, even if I don't always see where he's coming from. He would do well to admit more often that our systems are different.

Systemic confrontation

– But isn't he right when he calls for a more level playing field for our two parts of the world?

– Most of all, he has enough integrity to attract the attention of your fellow-Europeans to the fact that 61% of the Chamber's members now recognize that Chinese companies are as innovative as their European competitors. That's proof that our industrial policy pays off over time. Much more so than yours, which has ended up preventing a merger between the railroad construction operations of Siemens and Alstom, even though their combined size would still only be a third of the size of our giant China Railway Construction Corporation. Our system is the very opposite of the USA's. Theirs may well give more encouragement to invention, but it lacks strategic planning. Look at the largest American "tech" companies. With the notable exception of Microsoft, whose ability to reinvent itself never ceases to impress me, these huge groups are soon going to reach their limits: Facebook is going to get caught because of the way it uses personal data, and is incapable of competing on an equal footing with our TikTok; Alphabet will eventually be censured for being in a monopolistic position, and will be rivaled by Amazon in search monetization; Apple gets most of its growth from China, which accounts for 30% of its sales, and these are certain to fall in the future; Uber will be regulated one day; Tesla will turn out to be unable to raise its volume of production to the level its investors expect; Netflix will be cannibalized by the short-video explosion; Twitter will never manage to fully monetize its traffic; and Amazon will never make food home delivery profitable enough – and this is its main growth driver. So, I'm sorry to disappoint you, but the time is past when we had to look to the USA for our development. Americans have the arrogance to see our "tech" as a sort of Galápagos tortoise – a unique species that is unable to leave its own shores. You'll see, our "sea turtles" are going to be around for the next 200 years…

– And yet, every year, the USA pockets about $80 billion in royalties from industrial property, whereas you have to pay out a cool $23 billion. They still own 55% of global assets; you only have 15%.

– That's a legacy from the past. Luckily for us, they have ventured into an increased financialization of their ecosystem – the object being to conceal their industrial decline. The best example of this is the General Electric group, whose market capitalization has fallen from $600 to $100 billion in a few years. We believe the same fate will befall Boeing. Note that we were the first to ground the 737 MAX; your European regulator followed suit, and then the American Federal Aviation Administration. In 2019, the S&P 500 stock market index artificially benefited from $800 billion of share buybacks, a sum that will not now be invested in the future. Similarly, in 2019, over 75% of buyout transactions in the USA were only made possible by the dangerous leverage ratio of at least six times the EBITDA. The only way to justify excessive valuations. Have you read the definition of EBITDA – Earnings Before Interest, Taxes, Depreciation, and Amortization – in the loan docs for Del Fresco's Restaurant Group? It runs to 2,723 words – longer than the American Declaration of Independence which only has 1,338 words! The more time, energy and money the USA wastes on this financialization and legalism, the better for us.

– But, even if you see advantages in this systemic rivalry, isn't there a risk of companies relocating to Europe?

– I don't believe so for a moment. On the contrary, you Europeans are going to have to speed up your investment in China in order to help the "Made in China for China" focus. Take the example of the French-based world leader SEB, one of the very first forward-thinking companies to enter our market, and who made a takeover bid for Supor, our kitchen equipment manufacturer. SEB now has seven factories in Europe and seven in China, producing complementary lines. It has reduced the development time for its new products by 10% a year, and has three-phase product launches, two of which are scheduled six and 12 months after the initial product placement – this means that the competition is constantly taken by surprise. The Foxconn Group tried to keep President Trump happy by building an iPhone assembly factory in Wisconsin; my friend Terry Gou pocketed the huge amount of American subsidies and, in the end, just built a research center there because of the shortage of qualified workers in America. It's time you rebooted your brain's software and came to terms with the new reality: China is the source of future growth! Must I remind you of what has befallen your French friends? Their CAC40 had the same turnover in 2017 as in 2008. What's more, a study produced by the American Chamber of Commerce in Shanghai, in association with PwC, showed that, in April 2020, only 12% of the major American groups present in China who were interviewed had plans to relocate their own production to the USA, and only 24% planned to relocate part of their supply chain. Almost two-thirds of them had no plans to make any changes.

– I have to say that that is the case of my own group. We are planning to strengthen our supply chain here, but in a revolutionary way: using local applications engendered by blockchain. For example, it is our ambition to pre-finance our whole chain of subcontractors; in return, we want to get a complete oversight of their manufacturing process, with everything under blockchain control. In fact, in the space of ten years, the questions raised during Board meetings have changed completely. In 2009, my directors asked me, "What are the risks involved in going into China?" These days, they ask, "What are the risks involved in not going into China?"

– Ah, at last, a Board of Directors that actually does some work! Well, you can tell them from me to stop thinking that we're still dependent on the rest of the world. Our trade surplus is now no more than 1.7% of our GNP, as opposed to 8% in 2008; that's a lot less than major exporting countries like South Korea, whose surplus is still at 8%, or Germany with 5%.

– I understand your train of thought, but I must warn you that you might draw the wrong conclusions. Every time China has turned in on itself, it has foundered. Don't repeat the errors of the past. When, at the end of 2019, I heard about your new "3-5-7" rule for your state-owned companies, I was rather worried. Did you really want to force them to withdraw 30% of their foreign-made hardware and software by the end of 2020, 50% by the end of 2021 and 70% by the end of 2022? This cannot be the answer. On the contrary, we must seek greater cooperation in the flow of investment between China and Europe. In this way, we could help free you from the grip of the Americans. Remember: Europe has a huge wealth of knowledge.

Investing for good

– But we've always been open to your investment, and have continually shortened the list of strategic sectors barred to you. This is evidenced in the Comprehensive Agreement on Investment of December 2020.

– What's more, with your falling exports and the increased amounts your tourists are spending abroad, your balance of payments – which has usually shown a surplus in the past – will soon show a deficit. You're going to need our capital. That's why you're falling over yourselves to have your stock exchanges included in the MSCI Asia index. But foreign input is not just a financial issue, it could and should be an industrial issue too. Did you know that a third of all technological discoveries worldwide still come from Europe?

– That's why, on 1st January 2020, we brought laws governing foreign companies in line with those governing Chinese ones. This was in response to your requests and in order to facilitate your arrival. Do I need to remind you that your country's total investment in China is highly disproportionate to our investment in Germany? It was BASF – also from Germany – that made the biggest ever direct foreign investment in China in the summer of 2018 – €10 billion. This doubled the amount of the capital that it had engaged in China for over 20 years. Your car manufacturers – Volkswagen, BMW and Daimler – make almost half of their global profits on our market. Surely you must see that this is better than being subject to arbitrary taxation in the USA – $20 billion in the case of Volkswagen, $10 billion for Bayer.

– And this foreign investment is just as profitable for you, for these foreign companies account for 3% of businesses, 10% of jobs, 18% of corporate tax revenue, and over 40% of your country's exports. Look, even the greatest Chinese successes have benefited from foreign shareholders who have played a vital role: the South African Naspers in the case of Tencent, and the Japanese Softbank for Alibaba. And even look at ByteDance – the holding company that owns TikTok and Douyin. 80% of its shareholders are foreign – including KKR, Softbank, Sequoia, General Atlantic and Hillhouse – and five of its directors are not Chinese. Proof enough that foreigners can invest for good in China!

– Whereas there are seven Chinese nationals among the directors of companies on the S&P 500 index and only eight on the FTSE 350. I leave it up to you to work out which "ecosystem" is more closed to outsiders. Furthermore, in a study published in 2019, the McKinsey Global Institute underlined that, for the 10 largest categories of consumer products and taking account of only the 30 leading brands, foreign brands had a 40% market share in China in 2017, as compared to only 26% in the USA. In the beauty and personal care sector, it was even 73%!

– Yes, it's true that a good many multinationals will admit privately that your market is the most attractive in the world. Usually, these companies have put in the necessary human and financial resources to make sure they're not just there "to plant radishes" – to use the phrase often used by Antoine Riboud, the legendary chairman of Danone. But, even so, that doesn't change the fact that smaller companies encounter numerous problems when it comes to making acquisitions in China: double book-keeping makes the analysis of accounts more of an art than a technical skill; liability guarantees are ineffective when there are no escrow accounts in Hong Kong, because of your exchange control under the authority of your SAFE agency; asset deals are not worth it because of capital gains tax; and earn-outs are a headache to set up.

– Herr Doktor, do you want me to roll out the red carpet for foreign investors? Very well, but you'll have to agree that the CCP logo will be woven into it!

– Don't forget that, over the next 20 years, your industrial fabric will have to face up to the problem of who will succeed to your entrepreneurs of the eighties and nineties. Many of my Chinese suppliers are worried by the prospect of their only child not being interested in taking over operations. We Germans are experts in passing on small family businesses from one generation to the next, so you might benefit from our involvement, and potentially get help from the investment funds of your municipal authorities. From my experience, they keep their ear to the ground and this makes them very wise investors.

– Indeed, China is a highly decentralized country and is much more in the hands of local decision-makers than Westerners think. Our two countries are very alike in this respect.

– But, on the other hand, when Chinese entrepreneurs arrive in Germany to invest, we always see the hand of Beijing behind it. Your chaos management is very ineffective at an international level and leads you into absurd situations… For example, in 2016-2017, the Gang of Four companies Anbang, HNA, Wanda, Fosun were only too happy to pay over the odds for assets as diverse as the Waldorf Astoria and Hollywood studios in the USA, and for Deutsche Bank, Dufry, Gate Gourmet, Thomas Cook and Sonia Rykiel in Europe! Not to mention when ChinaChem purchased the Swiss company Syngenta for over $40 billion, and when Geely bought shares in Daimler when the market was at its peak!

– Yes, but we've learnt from our past mistakes and when our sportswear leader the Anta group took over the Scandinavian company Amer, we took care to finance almost all of the acquisition by a zero-coupon convertible loan… mainly underwritten by Western investors. This was a truly industrial project: over a period of 10 years, Anta has already multiplied by five the turnover of Fila, a company whose potential was ignored by Western investors. We are most grateful that you allow us to jump on such fine opportunities, as during the last football World Cup in Russia when your political boycott enabled us to snap up 35% of advertising space at unbeatable discount prices!

– I have no doubt that your opportunism will continue to work wonders from time to time. I am endeavoring to do the same, on a more modest level, within my own group. I'll let you into a secret that I should really keep to myself: have a close look at technology in France where 80% of "tech" companies with a turnover in excess of $50 million are now in the hands of foreigners, because of the lack of local financing. For us, this is a fabulous mine of know-how. But, looking beyond my own company, I'd like to convince you that our two parts of the world should think about a long-standing cooperation, for it's obvious that we complement each other.

Long-standing cooperation?

– I would like nothing better, but I'm afraid your political leaders in Europe don't share your point of view. They talk about nothing but "reciprocity", and yet we are offering them access to a market of 1.4 billion consumers.

– I totally agree with you. What really matters is the complementarity of value chains. In the 20th century, the best example of collaboration between the USA and Europe was the joint venture between General Electric and Safran – CFM International – for the construction of aircraft engines. The fact that they complemented each other perfectly has meant that the collaboration has stood the test of time.

– And how do you see Europe and China complementing each other?

– I would say that China excels in what is already known, and Europe is at its best in the unknown. Your ability to put things into execution combined with our imagination would be a combination with as much explosive potential as that of nitro and glycerine!

– And how do you see things on a practical level?

– You've been successful in industries where there are economies of scale, and we've gained leadership in sectors based on "ecosystems". You've become the world leader in solar panels and, according to IHS Market, you increased your share in the global market from 26% in 2010 to 82% in 2020, because the incredible volumes that you produce have made it possible to reduce the cost base, bringing it to parity with traditional energy sources. Even the Siemens conglomerate, albeit with one of the largest market capitalizations in Europe, recently took the historic decision – under the leadership of its iconoclastic CEO, Joe Kaeser – to split the group into three divisions: healthcare, energy and automation. He realized that it was no longer big enough to be an independent rival to your giant companies, and, for each sector of operations, had to envision mergers. He should be congratulated! On your side, over the last 20 years, you've put over $150 billion of subsidies into semi-conductors – a sector that is the perfect example of an "ecosystem" – but have nevertheless not managed to catch up with the West. An "ecosystem" needs trust in order to function, and that's what you are lacking most. How can knowledge be shared between all those involved in a value chain if they don't trust each other?

– Things change. In the summer of 2020, we engineered a

huge increase of over $6 billion in the capital of our "national champion" SMIC – Semi Conductor International Corporation – which we have put in charge of federating the whole industry.

– And I'm willing to bet that all this will achieve is the ruin of a few more savers in Shanghai. Oddly enough, the secret of success with semi-conductors lies not so much in their design as in their manufacture, which is not only extremely complex – with 1,200 successive steps – but is also constantly evolving. This is what will always be the stumbling block that prevents you from making up for the years you've lagged behind your Taiwanese and American competitors. You would do much better to specialize in design, just as Huawei has done with its Hisilcon operations, as well as in assembly and testing by cooperating with our European leaders Infineon or STMicro. The latter has managed an impressive turnaround precisely because of new management and a new strategy: a few years ago, they at last decided to focus on the opportunities offered by your domestic market. It is only by associating yourselves with European players that you will have any chance of rivaling the USA.

–Which other sector do you think we could cooperate in?

– Software and computer services. You'll never make up for lost ground with respect to the USA if you go on spending five times less than it does. In 2020, Goldman Sachs reckoned that your domestic computer services market was worth only $30 billion; that's barely 4% of the global market, which is worth $715 billion. The services sector accounted for only 11% of your total expenditure on IT, in comparison with 32% in the rest of the world – a result of your taste for hardware. And your leading computer companies – such as Chinasoft, Kingsoft and Kingdee – are of marginal importance globally. The top ten computer services companies worldwide have only 25% of the market, as compared to 40% for those that market software. So, the game's not over by a long chalk, and there's a real opportunity to be seized. Gartner estimated that, in 2020, 72 % of global expenditure on computer services was put to use as follows: 18% in banking, 18% in manufacturing, 16% in the media, 7% in insurance, 7% in distribution, 4% in healthcare and 2% in education. So, you can see that, in a number of sectors that are still under-penetrated, you might surprise the USA if we were to collaborate in the field of IT. We should focus our common efforts on the fastest-growing sectors, such as CRM – Customer Relationship Management – or Business Analytics. Don't waste your time developing your own solutions. Bear in mind that, when it comes to technology, it's the dog-years principle that prevails: one year behind is the equivalent of seven years in established industries. So stop letting each of your state-owned conglomerates develop its own internal IT services division just because of its supposed strategic importance – it'll be ineffective in any case. You'd do better to subcontract the services out to real global leaders, built with the help of European experts, and using local English-speaking staff, as they've done in India.

– I have to say that you put forward a convincing argument. Are there any other sectors you would prioritize?

– Industries involved with the environment and energy-saving. The USA's lack of industrial policy in these sectors is going to leave it a generation behind if we cooperate efficiently. Following your official policy, you're creating extra capacity in renewable energies. This is extremely impressive, but you're still having trouble linking them to your distribution network, not to mention organizing marketplaces to handle inter-regional trading of this production which is intrinsically volatile. The International Energy Agency estimates that 50% of the technology you will need in order to reach carbon neutrality by 2060 doesn't exist yet. So, let's collaborate! Let's take another sector: logistics. Isn't it interesting that the Bolloré group, one of the European leaders, has made an alliance with your Alibaba rather than with an American giant? But, more generally speaking, think above all about the industrial production that the USA abandoned almost 20 years ago – it fell victim to the "fabless" fashion. As our new European Commissioner for the Internal Market, Thierry Breton, said Europe is the world's leading industrial power. There are only 14,000 software engineers with General Electric, whereas Bosch has 20,000 and Siemens 21,000. During the 2010s, your combined technology imports from Japan and Germany – respectively 17% and 11% of the total – were almost the same as those from the USA – 27%. So, don't let Uncle Donald's provocations become a fixation. Your future depends on alliances like the ones made between Bosch, Kuka, Midea and Xiaomi over the connected objects of the future.

– Don't worry, we definitely intend to reduce our dependency on the USA, and the USA is about to discover how dependent it is on us. In the spring of 2020, the excellent report of the Boston Consulting Group, *How Restrictions to Trade with China could end US Leadership in Semi-Conductors,* showed only too well how the US market share in the semi-conductor sector – currently 50% – could fall by eight points if it maintains the restrictions it imposed on us with its famous "entity list", and by 18 points if it were to ban the sale of American technology to China. According to the Boston Consulting Group, any such policy would benefit Asia, in particular South Korea, which controls 24% of the global market and could well take first place.

– But it's almost certainly in the automobile industry that our collaboration could be most beneficial. At the moment, I believe you are going down the wrong path, when I hear your biggest real estate promoter Evergrande say that it wants to become the world's leading producer of electric vehicles, by incurring debts to the tune of tens of billions of dollars. The race to produce more and more is not the key to the future, now that the global market has undoubtedly reached its peak. I think rather that the most significant disruption to the sector will not come from technology but from consumer use. This will define what future models will be like. Contrary to the most optimistic predictions, the electric car market won't take off in any spectacular fashion, because we'll have to wait until 2030 or 2035 before the price of electric cars reaches parity with cars with combustion engines. Their price has done nothing but increase over the years, due to the increased autonomy demanded of the batteries. The average price is $51,000, still 44% above that of a car with a combustion engine.

– I can only agree with part of your analysis. Of course, like you, I'm not sure that the market in China for private cars will show any significant increase in the future over and above the 20 million that are currently sold every year. Electric cars will be too polluting given the amount of carbon in our electric power mix. They will also be excessively heavy, and the density of our population will limit ease of recharging. But my people are showing such a keen interest in them that I wouldn't be surprised to see Morgan Stanley's predictions come true. Their experts foresee a massive progression of electric vehicle sales, from 5% of all new vehicles sold in 2020 to almost 40% in 2030. But this industry will mainly prosper in two niche markets: the high end – in which our national leader NIO fully intends to rival the Californian Tesla – and "the last mile" for deliveries.

– The real revolution will be in shared use. In the 20th century, cars were only used to an average of 4% of the maximum usage for which they were designed. As regards the future "winner", I wouldn't put my money on Evergrande, but rather on the new Links brank that your Geely group, in alliance with Daimler as well, is developing in collaboration with Volvo. Its design, made with the aid of artificial intelligence, is based on the type of mobility that consumers will want, and focuses on the different sorts of shared use, which already accounts for 10% of demand in China. You will find exactly what you need in design software like that developed by the brilliant minds of Dassault Systèmes, the world leader. This software makes it possible to manufacture custom cars, produced in limited editions, by means of a basic platform available on the marketplace and open to all designers. Yet another reason to look towards Europe!

– Well, a long time ago, one of our most promising automobile groups, Brilliance, did the right thing in allying itself with BMW for private cars. More recently, it has made an alliance with Renault for utility vehicles.

– Ah yes, at the time I admired my friend Carlos Ghosn for managing to get Brilliance's past operations valued at zero and to have the joint venture recapitalized equally by Brilliance and Renault. Proof that you can only get the best possible agreement with China if you know how to "talk tough"!

– You didn't talk enough about the environment. I like to say that the traffic lights in China should be both red – for reform of the Party – and green – for the environment. How do you see Europe playing a role in financing this when I am told that 85% of our investment will have to be financed by the private sector?

– Welcome to green finance! In the field of energy and in terms of global consumption, you consume a quarter of the oil, half the coal, and account for at least a third of total investment in clean energy. Therefore, it's only natural that you should become the leading market in green finance. First of all, you could enter into closer collaboration with those European companies who are active in the Breakthrough Energy Coalition, which has set itself five priorities: energy storage, liquid fuel, the new energy grid, new construction materials, and geothermal energy. Then, you should follow the example of the Italian luxury goods group Prada, which was one of the first to sign a "green" loan with an interest rate that will vary according to compliance with environmental criteria selected and monitored by the lenders. More broadly speaking, what we have called "Impact Investing" has already shown significant positive effects in the areas of clean energy and agriculture, but has been less effective in healthcare and education. Those, I believe, are the two sectors in which you certainly have a role to play – with traditional Chinese medicine and online job training, for example.

– I'm afraid it's almost time to bring our conversation to an end, but let me go back to what I see as the main point. You are proposing a marriage of convenience – what the French call a "marriage of reason" between two economic players, China and Europe, which I would like to call "EuraXia". It was the French writer Sacha Guitry who said, with typical wit, "Marriage is rarely a marriage of reason – but a divorce is always a divorce of reason: you know each other by then." I believe that my priority should therefore be to have our peoples begin by getting to know each other better. The more they appreciate each other, the more chance there is of reason prevailing over the misconceptions we may have today. I would like to thank you warmly with a very special gift – a photo of your father shaking hands with Deng Xiaoping in 1979. Your father was an amazing visionary. Back in the late 1970s, he already saw the full potential of China, and he was one of the first European industrialists to take a gamble on us. I am delighted to see that his visionary side has not skipped a generation. And now, it is for the next generations that it is up to us to lay the foundations of our "EuraXia" of the future.

6

Friday – Hangzhou, at the head office of Alibaba, Magnus Flatpackson

"If you don't accept technology, you'd better go to another place, because no place here is safe."
Robert Rauschenberg

– My dear Magnus, thank you for joining me in the main monitoring room of the "Alibaba and his forty disruptors" group! What you see on the wall there is an immense planisphere with thousands of diodes that flash on and off every second. Each one represents a real time delivery of an Alibaba order somewhere in the world, showing us the reality of the company's "Global Circle of 1-2-3 Logistics" vision: one day to deliver to China, two days to deliver to neighboring countries, three days to deliver to any city in the world. And from this window, do you see those young saplings? Each one has been planted by a member of staff who has asked for a parking space for his or her car. This is the image of the New China that I wanted to show you: technological, environmental and global. My invitation must have surprised you, even though everyone has probably wanted to meet you ever since *Forbes* magazine put you on their worldwide 30 under 30 list. Naturally, I am eager to hear your views on the current digital revolution. I am equally intrigued by your choice to invest for the Wallenberg family office from a base in Stockholm rather than emigrate to the USA as most ambitious people in your field usually do.

– President Xi, I have to say that this interview is something quite out of the ordinary for me. I never meet politicians and I'm not familiar with what is politically correct, so please forgive me in advance for anything I say that might offend. We talk straight in the tech world. Let me begin by saying that I am proud to be Swedish, because my country is very often in advance of the rest of the world, although the rest of the world doesn't always realize it. In 1950, we were the first to recognize the People's Republic of China, and today we have been the first to remind you of our attachment to what we regard as universal values: we shall always defend this legacy of our Nobel Prize, even if, regretfully, this means that we have had to close all the Confucius Institutes in Sweden. Second only to Japan, we are the country that has the most unfavorable opinion of yours – and your ambassador has played a large part in this. I have agreed to this interview in the hope of persuading you that the future of China lies in a better relationship with Northern Europe, whose assets go largely unrecognized by the rest of the world.

– My dear Magnus, let me assure you that our conversation will not touch on politics, but rather on your specialty – the digital revolution, that you seem to have anticipated better than anyone. And, since you believe in straight talking, let me warn you in turn that, before following any advice you may give me, I go by the Baron Rothschild's healthy principle: "There are three main ways to lose money: wine, women, and engineers. While the first two are far more agreable, the third is far more certain."

– In one way or another, we are all entering the era of the VCs – the "venerable clots" or venture capitalists. We have to choose to be one or the other…

– You're forgetting the venture communists, the ones I want to be the big winners of the era.

Disintegrating the value chain

– Nice expression. It relates to my conception of the sharing economy that the digital world has brought about, and which I'm sure you will want to rechristen "Communism 4.0". Let me explain why I am as excited about it as my ancestors were in 1850 when they discovered the Industrial Revolution in Europe. The next decade will see the coming of the second digital wave, and it will transform the whole of the economy. Let's talk about the basics. Any business fulfils three essential functions: to create a product or service, to produce it, and to sell it. Therefore, we should think about how each of these three stages will be reshaped in the years to come. This is what I have called the "3D" revolution. It has three steps: first of all, the Disintegration of the value chain, then the Dematerialization of production, and lastly, the Disintermediation of distribution.

Money for value

– Let's start with disintegration. Where do you see this revolution of yours happening?

– Everywhere in the world! The main disruption of the 21st century – hardly ever mentioned even though it's the most important – is the population explosion. It's not climate change as my fellow Swede Greta will have it; she still hasn't understood that climate change is just one of the consequences of population increase. The answer to this problem can only come from technology, which can create a new lifestyle for an unprecedented density of population, particularly in urban areas.

– That's my main challenge, for although we only have a 50% urbanization rate, my country is already facing enormous environmental problems.

– And that's why the sharing economy is emerging; it's the only way of using resources efficiently. Bain, the strategy consultants, estimate that 100% of your growth in consumption will come from the sharing economy. And your enormous competitive advantage is that, culturally, you are much more prepared to share things: from an early age, you serve yourself from a common platter at mealtimes whereas, in the West, our food is served on individual plates.

– Maybe so, but surely it isn't in our instinct to want to share everything.

– Think again, because that's the biggest surprise of all. Take the example of AirBnB which has persuaded people from all sorts of backgrounds to share their own home – supposedly their most precious possession – with complete strangers. The American start-up investor, Bill Gross, now regrets that he missed out on the chance to invest in AirBnB at the very start. When he met the founders in 2007, he told them that his wife would never entrust a stranger with the keys of their New York penthouse with all its valuable paintings. But, in 2008, he was ruined overnight by the collapse of the financial markets after Lehmann Brothers went bankrupt and had to contemplate canceling his rental of the luxury island villa where, every year, he would go for a break at the end of September. His wife was despondent, so he had the wild idea of suggesting they should rent out their penthouse to finance the rental of the villa. He didn't hold out much hope that she would agree but, to his great surprise, she thought it was a brilliant idea. So you see that our propensity for sharing can change depending on the circumstances. The best bit of luck that the founders of AirBnB had was that the 2008 financial crisis came when it did.

– But how is that going to influence the creation of new products and services?

– They will just be designed for their true use. This is vital for your country, where consumers are and will remain the most demanding in the world. Traditionally, they only pay if they are satisfied. Take the case of medicine, for which your business model is the very opposite of ours: you only pay your doctor if you are in good health; when you fall ill, you stop paying him because he has obviously provided a bad service. We, on the other hand, are used to paying without thinking about the added value we receive. You are the winners with your "money for value" model, because you are paying only for the value perceived. In the West, however, we believe that the solution to any fall in our purchasing power will be "value for money". In our desperate search to make savings, we are constantly reducing the quality of our products and services, so we end up with horsemeat instead of beef on our plates.

– So you think that we Chinese have a cultural advantage over the USA?

– Definitely! The Achilles heel of Silicon Valley is that, basically, it tries to solve its own problems, that is to say the problems of the rich. It produced Uber, with a cost per mile of between $1.10 to $3.55. Where is the added value of this, except in cities where there is a lack of taxis? The real revolution has been in Europe with BlaBlaCar's carpooling, which has pushed the cost per mile down to 10 to 15 cents. The USA still lives in a bubble of 700 million privileged Westerners, whereas, for Europe and Asia, the digital revolution will involve a world of over seven billion people.

– I think we should expect the greatest benefits of this new approach to be felt in the healthcare industry, which you mentioned previously. Today, it's estimated that between 20 and 25% of medical procedures in hospitals are unjustified.

On average, it takes 10 years to develop any new drug, with only a 10% success rate; this leads to an astronomical development cost that averages out at $2.5 billion. Hardly money for value! I have to say that, personally, I think the big surprise of the Covid-19 crisis has been the discovery and manufacture of a new vaccine in under a year; beforehand, the whole industry said anything new took a minimum of three to five years to develop. And two of the revolutionary companies in the industry, BioNTech and Moderna, are headed up by Europeans – Turkish and French respectively.

– Tim Cook, the CEO of Apple, predicts that the field of healthcare is where his group will make the greatest contribution to humanity in the next 10 years.

– I think he's going to need it. I see that he's recently launched a new iPhone at $399, a lot less than the $1,000 he managed to charge his customers in the past. He's going to find out that your "money for value" has deflated – excellent news for my people's purchasing power.

– And I have some even better news for you. You've seen only the first ripple of the wave. In late 2019, Morgan Stanley carried out a fascinating study which showed that only three sectors of the economy had really been impacted by the digital revolution: media-telecommunications, commerce and tourism. These are the only sectors where the three main "disruptors" in the world have reached valuations that are higher than those of the three established leaders. Alphabet, Facebook and Tencent have beaten AT & T, Disney and Verizon; Amazon, Alibaba – our host today – and JD.com have beaten Walmart, Home Depot and Costco; Booking, AirBnB and Expedia have beaten Marriott, Hilton and IHG. In all the other sectors of the economy, the tidal wave is yet to come: in finance, education, healthcare, food, transportation, and business services. Note that Carlos Crespo, the new CEO of the fashion giant Inditex that owns the Zara chain, has a background in "tech", not in marketing; he is the former Chief Operating Officer of the group. The world's changing!

– You mentioned finance. What are your views on this sector?

TechFin, not *FinTech*

– Without doubt, finance is the industry that continues to ignore its customers the most. And it is in this area that it has to undergo a radical transformation. Newcomers to the sector are going to focus on the three most profitable operations: firstly, payment services; secondly, asset management; thirdly, and to a lesser degree, personal loans and loans to SMEs. The difference in approach between the West and China is that your existing services are so unsophisticated that newcomers can start from a blank page and develop what I call "TechFin". This means you invent a new sort of finance by means of technology – finance that I would describe as inclusive, because it aims to respond to the needs of all types of people, including the least well-off: the non-bankables. Western finance only seeks to change itself by FinTech, that is to say by developing new technologies that are simply grafted on to current finance, and only produce incremental improvements. And we still have 1,500 banks in Germany, 500 in Italy, 400 in France and 200 in Spain. So it's hardly surprising that none of them can impose any standard whatsoever on a global level.

– How do you see this industry developing in my country?

– At this stage, your biggest success is in your payment systems, where two newcomers – Alipay and WeChat Pay, subsidiaries of the ever-present Alibaba and Tencent groups respectively – have gained over 90% of the market in payments by cellphone, and have marginalized the established leader, UnionPay. They take a commission of about 0.5% as compared – in the West – to 2.6% for Square and 2.9% for PayPal. The moral can be seen in the result: Alipay has a billion users whereas PayPal has only 275 million after 20 years of existence. Your country has invented the cashless civilization, whilst the Mayor of New York is fighting to get retailers to continue to accept cash payments. 75% of Walmart's takings are still in the form of banknotes and coins.

– In Shanghai, even the vagrants – who are few and far between – accept contactless payment by Alipay!

– In the asset management sector, the Boston Consulting Group carried out a study in 2019 whose results estimated that, at the end of 2018, almost 50% of private assets for investment in China were still kept in the form of non-remunerated deposits, amounting to the colossal sum of 70,000 billion RMB – $10,000 billion. Two-thirds of your GDP! The Ant group, a subsidiary of Alibaba, very quickly attracted 1,000 billion RMB to its investment fund called Yue Bao – literally "forgotten treasure" – before the regulator put a curb on its rise. It's obvious that an annual growth of 15% in managed assets is to be expected in the next five years – half of global growth in the industry. This trend will continue over the long term, and it won't be reversed so long as the lack of real social protection continues to favor precautionary saving. According to the Bloomberg agency, only 7% of your compatriots have private health insurance, mostly because of a superstition that, once insured, they'll fall ill!

– Our hosts here at Alibaba have told me how they see asset management in the long term. They foresee interest rates remaining low for some time, which will naturally limit the levels of returns on savings. Therefore, they have devised a way to improve the quality of service which consists in personalizing each investment portfolio. Basing themselves on your purchases, which they know about by means of the Alipay payment system, they propose that you acquire shares in the companies that produce the goods and services that you buy. Rather than go by the often abstruse ESG-type criteria used in the West – "Environment, Society, Governance" –, they use big data to help you build up a portfolio of things you like. This will be the key to mobilizing personal savings in China – rather than American capital – to finance the future stock exchange flotations of our leading national companies.

– They are simply digitizing the martingale of one of the most successful US mutual funds of the 1960s. It was run by a group of elderly ladies who, during the day, went to supermarkets and noted what the best-selling products were. Their "investment committee" then got together every evening to exchange impressions.

– Those were the days when the USA still dominated the world's financial markets, but that's all over now. Already, in 2020, 45% of IPOs worldwide were launched on the Chinese markets, and $150 billion of foreign capital was invested here, predominantly in Treasury bonds. This influx followed the advice of Ray Dalio, the brilliant founder of the American Bridgewater fund, who, in December 2020, recommended to readers of the *Financial Times* that they should invest more in China, "a country that is weighted at only 3% in global funds, although it accounts for 15% of world GDP and a good third of its growth." So we are on the right track. But my question is a more general one: referring back to your elderly American ladies, is the coming technological revolution simply going to mean updating the past?

Online beats *offline*

– No, this new approach to any value chain is much more innovatory than you think. Bernard Charlès, the forward-looking CEO of Dassault Systèmes – that European jewel that is the envy of the Americans – explains it clearly: "The world is getting bigger. It is now made up of the real and the virtual, and they are interwoven. The real disruption is that reality and ideas become representable and accessible to everyone. The platformization of the 3D experience makes it possible to show how it really works and makes it intelligible for all the players." This reasoning is taking hold in all domains, going beyond industrial R&D and including services. What determines each one of my investments is my conviction that the new online experience beats the offline experience of the past. Take the sector of cultural showcasing. Dominique and Sylvain Levy, the founders of DSL Collection, want to rethink the whole thing. Owners of one of the major collections of contemporary Chinese art, this amazing French couple had the idea of not having their works go on tour in your museums – many of which are empty – but of simply displaying them online, starting mostly with some massive installations that digitization makes it possible to see from all angles and all distances. I think it's an admirable solution to the logistical headache of managing the numbers of visitors that a landmark exhibition would attract in a country like yours. It's obvious that we need a new digital broom to sweep our Western museums clean.

– I have noticed the same revolution in sporting events. E-sport will be recognized for the first time as an official discipline at the Asian Games in 2022. The post-lockdown period in the spring of 2020 following the Covid-19 crisis has simply hastened this revolution: in the space of six weeks, a host of digital applications appeared, offering all the services needed to encourage people to get back to a normal life: traceability, personal identification, contactless interaction, temperature checks, geolocalization of high-risk places, mobility flow management, teleworking, robotized delivery… I was staggered by the speed at which all these new services appeared. For me, this is something that will have a key role to play in the future for, as you know, we want at all costs to avoid the nightmare scenario of the notorious middle-income trap. Going from an economy driven by its industrial exports to one based on services has been tricky for many countries. Initially, the low productivity rate of new services endangers the new balance. Timewise, we are lucky in that we are going make this dangerous crossing at the very moment when services all over the world are being digitized faster and faster, with huge jumps in productivity.

– The Covid-19 experience has not been disruptive, that's for sure. Far from it. It has served to speed up the thrust of digitization, to the advantage of forward-looking companies like Alibaba and Tencent. But I don't think that governments and investors have as yet understood its significance. My highly-respected counterparts in Andreessen Horowitz measure the success of a start-up by how fast its innovatory idea is accepted in relation to the speed at which its established competitors can innovate. In our post-Covid world, it's the adoption of new forms of digitization that is tending to speed up most, and that's good news for start-ups.

– But how do you as an investor manage to identify so-called good ideas that aren't good at all, and worm out the lame ducks to be avoided?

– The classic response used to be to look at cash outflow, but things are more complicated than that these days. Your "disruptor" compatriots are used to following the precept "First destroy, then rebuild". Having raised excessive funds with the help of the current liquidity bubble, they cut prices so much that their competitors are brought to their knees, thereby creating "communities" whose value can initially be decorrelated from the company's economic performance. Don't forget that Amazon "squandered" $1.1 billion before reaching break-even in 2002. For me, the acid test is the gross profit, which reflects the real value harvested from disintegration of the value chain. That is what will guarantee your future, once the price war is over. This type of analysis makes it possible to avoid traps like WeWork – which managed to collect $12 billion in 12 successive fund-raising operations.

– Their scam even went as far as the improbable mention in their stock flotation prospectus of a "community-adjusted EBITDA" as one of the criteria for evaluating its profitability. I remember smiling when WeWork was revalued in the USA from $76 billion down to a "mere" $10 billion in seven days! It's a mystery to me how major international investors continue to have any confidence whatsoever in American investment banks and their infinite intellectual flexibility.

– Extreme vigilance is the order of the day, particularly with regard to newcomers to the stock exchange, 80% of which are companies making losses. These pseudo-unicorns, with highly respectable turnover levels, promise you that, because of their operating leverage, you will make a profit that, in most cases, you will never see. The lower economic profile of their marginal customer, given decreasing revenue together with ever-increasing acquisition costs, encourages them to go cap in hand in search of incessant recapitalizations. In your part of the world, you have had utterly nonsensical examples like Ofo's discount bicycle rental venture or Luckin Coffee, which aimed to rival Starbuck's by offering free coffee. Both went out of business and lost several billions of dollars. So, more than ever, *caveat emptor*!

– Do what I do, give your trust sparingly!

– Exactly. Trust is something that digitization will also help to redesign. But for that, we first need to talk about the second "D" of the "3D" revolution. Having Disintegrated the value chain in order to design a product, we now have to Dematerialize its production.

Dematerializing production

– As you know, China is seen these days as the "workshop of the world". That's what's made it possible for us to "take off" during the last 30 years. So I'm eager to understand how the production of goods and services is going to be transformed.

– Let's start from a very simple idea: data will not merely be the oil of the 21st century; more importantly, it will also be the tool of a new form of colonization, with the enormous advantage that no physical movement is necessary. For you, who always make a point of the fact that you have never invaded anyone, this is an opportunity not to be missed!

It all comes down to data

– Our national guru, my friend Kai-Fu Lee, who wrote the "bible" *AI – Superpowers*, regularly keeps me up to date with how his work is progressing. He still thinks that, over time, we Chinese are building up a competitive edge over the West because of our mass of data and an absence of the sort of regulations that force you to work in isolation in ivory towers. So we're going to be able to find unexpected correlations that will considerably reduce the cost of acquiring this data, and will give our service providers a vital competitive edge. Kai-Fu Lee quotes the example of consumer credit which, in the West, has always been based on statistics such as monthly income. In China, however, it is extremely difficult to obtain this information because it isn't always reliable. This is because of the size of the underground economy and the role played by families. Kai Fu Lee has had the brilliant idea of using "alternative data", namely the level of charge of your smartphone battery at different times of the day. If, each time it is measured, the level is above 50%, Kai-Fu Lee will agree to lend you money, because your aversion to risk indicates the likelihood of your paying back the loan. For you in the West, this sort of "alternative data" is private; in order to get hold of it, your companies would have to resort to external databases, and the cost of doing this would be prohibitive.

– Your reasoning appeals to the intellect but, unfortunately for you, the facts don't bear it out. Alipay has paid dear with its Sesame credit scoring system, and has had to admit publicly that the scheme has limited usefulness. In the same way, Lufax, one of the FinTech operations of the insurance giant PingAn, has collected financial data on 150 million Chinese and non-financial data on almost 450 million of them. It now admits that 90% of its decisions to grant loans are determined by financial data alone. This is because it's all about the quality of the data, which can vary widely according to whether it's "structured" as is often the case in the West, or "non-structured" as is usually the case in China. I recommend that you look at *Spurious Correlations* by Tyler Vigen, which shows a number of perfect statistical correlations between two data sets with no logical connection. For example, you will find the perfect relationship between, on the one hand, American expenditure on science, space and technology and, on the other hand, the number of suicides by hanging, strangulation and suffocation!

– That correlation seems perfectly logical to me if overpaid researchers are finding it increasingly difficult to discover anything!

– It's already very difficult to draw reasonable conclusions from structured data; with unstructured data, the challenges ahead are inestimable. Let me tell you about the unfortunate thing that happened in 2018 to a European delegation that was invited by the Mayor of Shenzhen to take part in a discussion about political infrastructures. The group of senior civil servants had a very constructive exchange of views with their Chinese counterparts during the day and returned to Hong Kong in the evening. One of them was retained at the border for two hours and, when he was finally released, he explained to his colleagues: "This is the third time I've been to China. The first time was in June 2010, the second in June 2014. For two hours they've been asking me why I come to spy on China every time there's a football World Cup!" This is why, as any good European investor would, I prefer smart data to big data!

– My turn now to be skeptical about your theoretical thinking. Like any good Chinese, I am a pragmatist. Look at the Tencent group. It has developed an AIMIS – an AI Medical Innovation System – in the field of medical imagery. The system has already interpreted over a hundred million images and diagnosed over a million patients, at a fraction of the cost of a Western medical service. And look at our friends Alibaba. Having dematerialized e-commerce, they are now dematerializing computer infrastructure on the cloud, making it accessible to all small businesses in China. This transformation is only at its early stages, because the cloud is estimated to have penetrated only 10% of the market as yet. Image recognition is going to produce a whole range of new applications, like those that make it possible to find out where your jacket came from and, in an instant, to buy one just like it online.

– I am questioning not the expected benefits, but rather any systematic competitive edge to be gained from your economies of scale – I think this is too optimistic a supposition. First of all, your system has "dis-economies" of scale, for any private company above a certain size goes in fear of state supervision. Furthermore, in Europe, it is the tiny country of Estonia – once again, follow my advice and take a closer look at Northern Europe! – that has been the most agile in turning a large number of everyday administrative procedures into online services for its people.

– But Estonia has only a million and a half inhabitants! A mere district! I have 1.4 billion people to deal with here!

– Agility is more important than size these days: medical prescriptions, electronic signing, online voting, blockchain for public registers, etc. You'll see, you'll be surprised by the increased productivity of your public services once they're digitized… I agree with you insofar as this "data revolution" will be in four stages that we will have to come to grips with one after another; first of all, data collection, which we have already talked about; secondly, understanding the data – called "insight" by the specialists – using artificial intelligence; thirdly, visualization, in which augmented reality will play a large part; and, finally, implementation, in which automation will take the lead.

– That's why he who masters artificial intelligence will dominate the world. And that's why our regulations on data will focus on the potential dangers of private companies getting monopolies, whilst you Europeans are going to get entangled in the problems involved in the protection of personal data. Our NDRC – the National Development and Reform Commission – has already identified the opportunities: it is banking on the Chinese market in "Core AI" progressing from $23 billion in 2020 to $62 billion in 2025 and $154 billion in 2030. Given the spillover effects on to other sectors, the market opportunity is gigantic, rising from $150 billion in 2025 to $1,550 billion in 2030. The industries most heavily impacted will be healthcare, automobiles, security and industrial automation. As the CEO of Baidu, Robin Li, says: "The internet was just the starter, artificial intelligence is the main course." And where in the world do you think these applications are going to be developed first, when 90% of young Chinese see artificial intelligence as something positive and trust robots more than their bosses, and when 73% of them would rather lose their wallet than their cellphone?

AI: the alternative intelligence

– The big difference AI will make when it arrives is machine learning: the ability of a machine to learn by itself from the data it processes. You may have read the fascinating conversation between Henry Kissinger, a great friend of China, Eric Schmidt, the former CEO of Google, and Dan Huttenlocher, the Dean of Schwarzman College of Computing at MIT. Their conclusion was that, "The challenge of absorbing this new technology into the values and practices of the existing culture has no precedent. The most comparable event was the transition from the medieval to the modern period. In the medieval period, people interpreted the universe as a creation of the divine and all its manifestations as emanations of divine will. When the unity of the Christian

Church was broken, the question of what unifying concept could replace it arose. The answer finally emerged in what we now call the Age of Enlightenment, great philosophers replaced divine inspiration with reason, experimentation, and a pragmatic approach. Other interpretations followed: philosophy of history; sociological interpretations of reality. But the phenomenon of a machine that assists – or possibly surpasses –humans in mental labor and helps to both predict and shape outcomes is unique in human history. The Enlightenment philosopher Immanuel Kant ascribed truth to the impact of the structure of the human mind on observed reality. AI's truth is more contingent and ambiguous; it modifies itself as it acquires and analyzes data."

– I like your analogy with the Middle Ages, for it is precisely at the end of that period of history that China began to break away from the West, and not in the mid-19th century as our official propaganda would have it. We should go back to square one – the Middle Ages; that would give us even more chance of reconquering world leadership. This is what the NRDC has already done, by assigning a specific sector to each of our national leaders: the smart city for Alibaba, healthcare for Tencent, self-driving cars for Baidu, voice and face recognition for iFlytech, logistics and drones for JD.com. The initial short-term focus will be on voice and face recognition – with Sensetime also contributing – so as to develop the simplest of applications such as Smile and Pay, when all you have to do is smile at a camera. Other projects such as the self-driving car will not be completed until 2030, but will see a huge value shift, if the software accounts for half of a car's value.

– I'm still a little skeptical about your chances in this domain, because I'm afraid self-driving vehicles will be the only ones that stick to the driving laws in China!

– Whatever happens, it will be in China that the driving experience will be reinvented. That's already the underlying philosophy of the partnership agreement between Huawei and the PSA Group – a good illustration of our desire to work with European industry. Also, blockchain will bring new thinking on the logistics of supply chains and eventually provide any required traceability. As one Western banker summed it up so well, "At the end of the day, during the 2008 crisis, you found out that your banker had landed you with a subprime that you didn't know existed; during the 2020 crisis, you found out that your supplies from China depended on a pangolin that you didn't know existed either!" That's what blockchain is going to avoid in the future. It's going to make it possible to restore confidence, including in new areas like digital currency where we intend to emerge as world leader, because its credibility won't derive from the issuer – the independence of the US Federal Reserve Bank is just an illusion –, but from the use that is made of it, and that use will be controlled by blockchain.

– And that will mark the return to companies investing in their IT infrastructure. Experts from Morgan Stanley point out that the infrastructure share of IT investment reached a plateau of about 30% during the boom of the year 2000. The IT revolution has moved from the desktop internet of the first decade of this century to the mobile internet of the second decade. The digital manufacturing revolution is preparing to marry R&D to IT. These are two departments which used to work separately in their own ivory towers, but are now going to have to collaborate on a daily basis. That was the original idea behind the very promising buyout of the engineering group Altran by the computer services group Cap Gemini. Together, they intend to revolutionize manufacturing in the same way that Accenture has reinvented digitally-based communication over the last 10 years, disrupting the large established advertising agencies such as Omnicom and Publicis.

– I have asked to be kept up to date with the discoveries made by the new Innovation Center that Capgemini has just opened in the Greater Bay Area.

– You should have a particular interest in that because a recent McKinsey study asserted that fewer than 20% of your industrial companies have a real digitalization strategy of their production. Over the last decade, industrial investments have concentrated on real estate and aeronautics; in the coming decade, they will concentrate on automation and corporate software. Your companies are still sorely lacking in these powerful pieces of software, which remain in the hands of the Americans. It's worth noting that, in passing from the model of the license acquired for all time to that of subscription on request, in conjunction with the development of the cloud, four out of the five largest players – Microsoft, Oracle, Adobe and SAP – are established suppliers who still have almost half the market; the only newcomer being Salesforce. You will never manage to gain any significant place in the software industry if you go it alone.

– Let's suppose, for the sake of argument, that you're right. Where does one start?

– I'm prepared to bet that you'll be surprised by European digital know-how in the fields of automation, energy production – where digital still only accounts for less than 5% of investment –, smart grids and e-mobility. You'll see that, from being immobile, we're going to become e-mobile!

– I am delighted to hear it. In the meantime, I can see more surprises coming from my country with regard to the digitization of e-commerce, healthcare, logistics and, in the long term, automobile mobility. I see now that we complement each other much more than I had realized.

– And you will also discover our skills in coding, whilst you excel in application assembly. There too, we complement each other. Coding is naturally influenced by the desired objective, and requires considerable creativity and freedom of choice, which are the keystones of European culture. This is why I would rather speak of alternative intelligence than of artificial intelligence. Never forget the human element! The main weakness of AI is likely to be that it focuses on one single dimension at a time, missing the potentially harmful side-effects.

The internet of things or the internet of the people?

– But, ultimately, it is people who will benefit from the internet of things. As the Governor of Guangdong told me, his Greater Bay Area project aims to combine hardware and software to develop platforms of B2C as well as B2B services. Of course, future benefits are mainly expected to be in the B2B sphere, particularly in the industrial sector – forecasting, prevention, maintenance and restocking – but the same trend will apply to B2C. We see this already in the USA with Google buying up hardware companies in anticipation of the potential of the internet of things.

– But you'll still have to settle the problem of personal data one day or another. At this stage, as Chancellor Angela Merkel has pointed out, this sort of data is in private hands in the USA; in China, it is confiscated by the state; Europe has to invent a third way. I think the business model favored by Silicon Valley is going to have to change. Maximizing the operating leverage of software without human input is going to reach its limits. The next decade will see high priority given to the return of both humans and machines. The West will realize that "if the product is free, then you are the product". Hence the emergence of concepts like that of the data portfolio that makes it possible for each one of us to decide whether or not to allow a company to access our data for a fee. That's what I call "C2B" – Consumer to Business. For me, that will be the most realistic way of introducing a universal income that will be financed by the giants of data collection. Fixing the price will be a delicate matter, but the British-based weekly *The Economist* has had the idea of looking at the question the other way round: how much would you have to be paid for you to stop using your email, your social media WeChat or WhatsApp, or your search engine Google or Baidu?

– That would enable me to further the rebalancing of the economy by speeding up domestic consumption – particularly that of my 600 million rural inhabitants – without it costing the government a cent…

– Particularly since alternative intelligence is going to exacerbate inequalities by getting rid of a good many jobs with low added value, as well as some jobs with middling added value. I foresee that in the West – and this is eventually going to be your case as well – we will see "data cooperatives" along the lines of the workers' trades unions that emerged during the first Industrial Revolution. Resourceful start-uppers will collect personal data linked to specific themes and will broker them in bulk to those involved in those particular sectors. At the same time, companies will create the job of data purchaser, whose task will be to acquire data in the cheapest and most direct way possible. The disruptors of the first wave of the digital revolution will become the disrupted of the second wave!

– So you're saying that this will be the end of the reign of the GAFA – I like that!

– Not necessarily. It will all depend on whether the GAFA, like your Chinese giant companies, turn to Europe to supply their model with notions of ethics, regulation, protection and cybersecurity. One of the least acceptable aspects of the AI world is that 87% of the people involved are men. In years to come, *#MeToo* will gain a foothold in the "internet of the people" and, under pressure from women, a more balanced model will finally emerge.

– And how long do you think all these changes are going to take?

– If one is to believe the forecasts of Goldman Sachs: three or four years. In its report *New Infrastructure – The Next Five Years* published in the summer of 2020, the US investment bank estimates that, by the end of that period, heavy investment that is still to be made will have resulted in tangible profits. That seems to me to be a realistic prospect if you recall that a previous cycle saw Steve Jobs invent the iPhone in 2007, but sales only took off as from 2011-2012, once App Store had made almost 250,000 apps available. So, your internet users will have to wait until 2023-2024 before they can sing revolutionary songs in honor of the "the people's internet".

– Thank you for warning me. It gives me three or four years in which to put these developments under control.

– But, in the meantime, the third "D" of the "3D" revolution will also be happening – the Disintermediation of distribution.

Disintermediating distribution

– This is a field in which we in China are already far in advance of the rest of the world, notably the USA. E-commerce in China already accounts for 30% of sales. Alibaba's annual sales have reached the incredible sum of $1,000 billion – 15% of the country's total trade.

Direct to the consumer

– As usual, you have managed to turn a threat into an opportunity. Your traditional distribution system with up to five or six levels of middlemen needed in order to cover the whole of the country, worked so badly that it caused a backlash producing the fastest development of e-commerce in the world. It's been a long while since you adopted the "85/15, 15/85" rule that the West has not yet been able to apply everywhere. When e-commerce only accounted for 15% of sales, you were the first to understand that 85% of customer experience took place online. So, logically, you decided to focus your advertising on the new digital media. This triggered the upward spiraling of e-commerce.

– The Covid-19 crisis has led us to reconfigure all face-to-face interaction, for we've realized that it accounts for about a third of our economy. Online contact makes it possible to have a direct contact with the consumer when contact in the real world is getting increasingly difficult. The practical advantages of the internet are becoming well-established.

– And this explains the disappearance of the department store model. The diversity of what department stores provide is under attack from online aggregators of products and services who are even causing the websites of individual brands to disappear. The latter can no longer manage to attract enough customers when there is such an abundance of offers. An aggregator in the fashion industry is able to introduce up to 3,000 new articles every week, and this makes the simple act of purchasing something into a fun shopping experience. Gone are the middlemen.

– I realized that we were in advance of your Western model some time ago when Google invested $500 million in our distributor JD.com. This was proof that the Americans had something to learn from our online sales techniques. They are still at the e-commerce stage whereas, in the meantime, we have developed m-commerce for smartphones, and are now transforming this into social commerce. It is even the case that some of your large groups like L'Oréal and Nike continue to prosper because of WeChat, whereas they refuse to collaborate with Amazon. What's more, L'Oréal has paid us a special tribute by changing its managerial principle of "excellence" – a word symbolic of Western arrogance – to "agility" – an eminently Chinese quality.

– And these transformations have far more surprises in store. The next step is the arrival of "decentralized autonomous organizations" by means of which the "people's internet" will oust the marketplaces and put consumers in direct contact with each other by means of a trust-generating system based on blockchain, and payment in cryptocurrencies. The ultimate aim is selling "direct from the vendor to the consumer", and the consumer retains ownership of his personal data. It will be the turn of the marketplaces to be "disrupted", because they don't give enough added value. As investors, we will have to be more and more patient because any start-up will have to pass through four stages. First of all, defining the product; secondly, building up a community; thirdly, monetizing; and finally, making a profit.

– And, therefore, I imagine that for you this means bringing costs down to a minimum, a necessity that these recent years of excessive liquidities tended to mask.

– Especially since our customers' purchasing power is going to become even more of a crucial issue. In the OECD countries, average real income increased by 27% between 1998 and 2008, but by only 8% from 2008 to 2017. Within the context of future budget constraints, welfare benefits won't have as much of a buffering effect as before.

– How do you think I should deal with the future problem of my people's purchasing power?

"Only half will do"

– By companies increasing their productivity. A few years ago, Procter & Gamble announced that it was going to reduce its global advertising budget by $2 billion – a budget that had reached the astronomical sum of $7 billion dollars at the time. It was beginning to understand the potential of merging its media and sales departments, which is what makes the social commerce of your Chinese networks possible. As always, you love to multitask and to mix things: your stores help build up your image, and your online messages on social media are directly integrated into your online sales. Retail becomes media, and media becomes retail. The increased productivity is obvious: it is estimated that it takes 0.9 employees to generate $1 million of online sales, whereas it takes 3.5 employees in a store. You'll see that technology will continue to be the main vehicle of transformation in the media industry. Remember that it was low-speed internet that initially transformed music consumption; then ADSL made video possible; broadband brought Netflix to the fore, eating into pay television; the next step will be 5G that will bring about the explosion of live streaming, video games and short-form video. Take the example of the search industry where, with the boom in connected objects, voice will predominate, causing voice recognition technology to revolutionize the advertising market. Not to mention video, which today accounts for 80% of content on Instagram, which was initially a professional platform designed by photographers for photographers.

– That's precisely why we are banking on our future technological progress, going beyond 5G, to surprise you in the media world, and to siphon off the $100 billion earned every year by the American media content industry…

– … with Europe as your source for new content. Tencent has taken a stake in Voodoo, the world leader in hyper-casual mobile video games – which originated in France – and which was valued at $1.4 billion when the transaction took place. In the future, you'll have control of the best distribution platforms and Europe will provide you with the most innovative content.

– I rather like this idea of cooperation in the content sector. I would be delighted to see our so-called dictatorship develop the future standards of global media.

– Don't forget that you can count on the fingers of one hand the number of major Chinese companies in the digital field that have actually earned a lot of money: Tencent, Alibaba, NetEase, Baidu and C-Trip. The rest of your "super-multicorns" may well have very impressive valuations, but these are based on multiples that only mean anything in the very long term, with a hypothetical profitability in the future that is totally disconnected from past performance. And the distribution platforms will depend on the content you provide in order to reach full power, hence the advantage of collaborating with Europe.

– That's exactly how we intend to benefit from the economies of scale that have served us so well in establishing our considerable lead in renewable energy.

– Personally, I see healthcare as holding the greatest potential for new business models. Even in the West, 80% of people are prepared to give out their personal data if that can contribute to medical research. The present cost of health services in the West is prohibitive and the failed attempt of a newcomer to enter the market in the USA – as unexpected as the alliance between Amazon, JP Morgan and Warren Buffet – proves that the solution is not going to come from current players in the economy, not even from the best among them.

– The mismanagement of your Western system can be explained by the fact that the patient doesn't pay for the service. In a country like France, only 7% of patients' expenditure is actually charged to them, whereas it is almost 30% in China. It's hardly surprising that 25% of nights spent in hospital could be avoided by dispensing treatment during the daytime. Our target is to achieve healthcare costs that are 50% lower than yours. We want to turn our human limitations – only 1.5 doctors for every 1,000 inhabitants – into an advantage. The insurer PingAn has estimated that, before the Covid-19 crisis, only 3% of visits to the doctor were virtual ones, whereas the long-term potential is 33%. Its subsidiary PingAn Good Doctor has developed the "Independent Advisory Room" and "Smart Medicine Cabinet" concepts that enable the patient to get a preliminary diagnosis from a doctor on the cloud, and to buy the most frequently prescribed drugs online.

– You should take the lead from my country, Sweden, where everyone can access their medical history on the internet.

Look at Northern Europe and forget America! And, more generally, give your logistics sector a complete makeover. Expressed in terms of GDP, it costs you twice as much as it does in Europe. In the fashion industry, 20% of the companies are taking 100% of the profits – they are the ones who have rethought their logistics and drastically reduced the product cycle to six to eight weeks, as compared to the average of forty weeks for the sector. Look at the case of Inditex in Spain if you want an insight into one of the most successful multichannel strategies – O2O: Online-Offline integration. But all these cost reductions we're talking about don't touch on the most interesting aspect of the second wave of the digital revolution.

– And what might that be?

– The greatest benefit to come from the digital revolution is what we are all seeking: the personalized offer to the customer.

"This time, it's personal!"

– Surely you're not going to ask my government to personalize decisions for each one of its 1.4 billion citizens! I have absolutely no desire to turn myself into an ice-cream seller, like some Western leader who has to hold a referendum to find out if people prefer vanilla or chocolate!

– I rather imagined that all the flavors you would have on offer would be red in color… But, in a country like yours, alternative intelligence can be used particularly well as a source of added value, enabling you to offer a targeted service for a very wide sector of the population who are submitted to an overabundance of offers. This is why 90% of Chinese people recently stated that they would be prepared to share their personal data in order to obtain a better customer experience. According to a survey commissioned by Unibail-Rodamco, only a third of Europeans would be prepared to do this. Note that even one of the best distributors in the world – Décathlon, a French company specializing in sports equipment – estimates that it is missing out on 20% of potential in-store sales because what it offers isn't tailored to its clientele. So you can see the potential of customer data!

– I can already see this in healthcare where one of our most successful companies, IcarbonX, will analyze your DNA so as to determine which drugs will suit you best or to suggest what food to eat – for a carrot won't have the same effect on you as it does on me. Likewise, we are the first to have made a dream come true for you and your investor friends: the personalized press revue, thanks to algorithms provided by Toutiao and which brought the ByteDance conglomerate such phenomenal success, including its brilliant development of the Douyin short-form video application, known abroad as TikTok. TikTok had such a stupendous success in the USA that President Trump stopped it out of hand. The ByteDance algorithms identify both your special interests and your emotional sensitivity. In this way they can identify what sort of person you are far better than any of your Western psychologists. And that's how ByteDance has gained 20% of the online advertising market in China in just a few years.

– You just have to look at the marriage sector in the USA. In making "the most important decision of one's life", one's choice can be influenced by a more extreme form of personalization. It is estimated that over a third of marriages are the outcome of a relationship that began online – 70% in the case of same-sex marriages. Traditionally, couples came together because of social class, location and parental influence. Now, there is considerably more freedom of choice, as shown in the increasing number of mixed marriages. More generally, the search market will be revolutionized, because it is finally going to become "intelligent" – a sort of GPS of knowledge. You and I will no longer get the same answer when we search for something on Google or Baidu. Furthermore, we will make less and less use of those search engines to look for a specific product, because that will have become the domain of the marketplaces – Amazon has already raked in over 10% of American online advertising. We are more likely to be asking for details of something we have experienced or how to solve a problem and, by definition, you and I will expect different answers. It is on this sort of precision targeting that future brands will build their offer, China included. Arnold Ma, CEO of the first Anglo-Chinese digital marketing company, Qumin, puts it like this: "Strategies based on simply pairing up marketing and sales don't work any more in China. Now that China has opened up more to the rest of the world, brand content is becoming the key." That's where you're going to need all our European know-how on building up a brand, once the race for distribution is over.

– You remind me of the waiters at the Caprice restaurant in the Four Seasons Hotel in Hong Kong. They have iPads that know what you ordered when you ate there last and, depending on what it was, they recommend you try one or other of the chef's new creations. You want to democratize this degree of service and bring it within the reach of all consumers. In this way, a true "Communism 4.0" will finally triumph and will give "to each according to his needs"! Death to 20th century capitalism which gave "to each according to his means"! My dear Magnus, I was sure that we would have a fascinating conversation, but I have the impression I've learned more about the digital revolution from you than from all my numerous meetings with the planning experts of the NDRC. With you, I get the impression I'm learning a new alphabet: A for AI, B for big data, C for cloud… I now have a better understanding of how the 2020s will be as "roaring" for China as the original "Roaring 20s" were for the USA a hundred years ago.

– I did warn you when we started this interview: our European brains are brimming over with ideas. You have the strike power of your distribution platforms; we can create innovative and attractive content. So let's combine our talents and put up a challenge to the Americans.

– As a token of my gratitude, may I offer you something that, up to now, I have never offered any foreigner: a month's free access to the Chinese Communist Party's mobile app. Every party member has to connect to it every day and over 80 million of them loyally do so. With all those billions in the funds of the Wallenberg family and their friends, I'm sure you'll want to make me an offer for it, but I'm sorry, our app is not for sale!

7

Sunday – Zhongnanhai, Politburo Standing Committee

Speech by Xi Jinping, General Secretary of the Chinese Communist Party

My dear comrades,

Thank you once again for giving up your Sunday to attend another special meeting I have convened. Last time, I promised to get back to you after my week of interviews with European experts from various backgrounds. I thought these conversations would confirm the opinions that I held and I was sure that they would also be full of surprises. In fact, they have made me change my position radically with regard to Europe. Remember our proverb: "When the wind of change blows, some people build walls and others build windmills." Today, we are lucky in that our enemy for years to come – the United States of America – has clearly chosen to build walls. Not just a physical wall on its border with Mexico, and not just a wall of competition preventing creative new ideas like TikTok from entering its market, but a cultural wall that America has decided to use in order to put an obstacle in the way of what China can bring to the rest of the world.

Against this background, I initially saw Europe as a declining reserve of resources to exploit: an area of trade surplus to bring in currency; a source of technology that we could gain hold of without encountering the same sort of resistance as we have had from the USA; an area of geostrategic influence that we could annex at little cost because of our effective control of its southern and eastern parts.

I have changed my mind. I think there is more to gain by setting up a cooperation with Chinese characteristics between our two ancient civilizations. Together, we could build new windmills, not built to Dutch specifications, but windmills built in Guangdong.

In the course of my conversations with these Europeans, I have realized that it is by playing on our complementarity that we can have more influence over them – complementarity that can be political, sociological, geopolitical, industrial and digital. Politically, Europe can learn a lot from us: the European democratic model can only survive if it goes back to the principle that any rights bring duties with them – the belief on which our national unity is based. From a societal standpoint, the rise of our new sharing society – "Communism 4.0" – will be the only way for Europe to mitigate the fall in its population's purchasing power. From a geopolitical standpoint, a *rapprochement* with Europe will strengthen our sphere of influence in Eurasia, beginning with the Iran-Turkey-Russia axis. From the industrial standpoint, I intend to study the European "ecosystem industries", which will be key factors in avoiding the middle income trap. Lastly, with regard to the digital revolution, I must admit that I hadn't taken the full measure of Europe's contribution to the Americans' success during the first wave. It is our turn this time to benefit from it – during the second wave. This is how my week of interviews has made me believe that our two continents can complement each other My objective now is to build a new China-Europe axis, a Eurasia that will strengthen our return to the world stage. I have called it "EuraXia".

However, I am a realist. What I am proposing will take a century to achieve. We are too advanced in years to hope to reap all of its benefits ourselves; it will be our grandchildren who, in 2100, will thank us for being so forward-thinking. In the 20th century, Europe and the USA joined in an alliance to create one camp – the West; in the 21st century, China and Europe will move closer together in order to build "EuraXia" together. Whereas Europe saw things in the 20th century through a simple eye-glass, we can provide it with a telescope that will give it a truly long-distance perception of the future and convince it that it is culturally much closer to us than to the USA.

I can already see tangible signs of this new situation in the short term. The path to "EuraXia" will not be a straight one, for Europe is just beginning to express the ambition to put its own house in order. But, by helping them to do this, we shall be able to access everything Europe gave America in the 20th century: its multiculturalism, its creativity, its *savoir-vivre*, and also its know-how, which has been largely underestimated.

However, we should remain realistic and be prepared to face a skilful combination of competition and confrontation under cover of cooperation.

We are lucky with the timing – a gift from Donald Trump that President Biden will find it difficult to make us return – because the break-up of the Western camp has come at a time when the second wave of the digital revolution is almost upon us. Three or four years from now, artificial intelligence will be changing the situation of industry as a whole, just as the steam engine did in 1850 during the Industrial Revolution. Past alliances will have to be reconsidered. Europe, hampered by the conservatism of its political class, will as usual look backwards through its rear-view mirror. So it is up to us to persuade its new generation of entrepreneurs that it's always best to go forward – and go east to "EuraXia".

There are moments when history seems to go faster – when the wheel turns. The last time this happened was in 1979, as the Lebanese writer Amin Maalouf says in *The Disoriented*: the elections of Margaret Thatcher and Ronald Reagan were the prelude to the resurgence of British and American liberalism; the Soviet Union's defeat in Afghanistan heralded its future collapse; the Islamic Revolution took place in Iran and Pope John Paul II began his pontificate… Above all, 1979 was the year when Deng Xiaoping gained full empowerment, marking our return to the world stage.

2021 should be an equally historic year, when we celebrate the centenary of the Chinese Communist Party. On that occasion, I intend to rebaptize it the "Chinese Civilization Party" and to leave my mark on this "beginning of history" by launching the "EuraXia" project.

I give you the coming week to come up with concrete proposals to this effect, in each of your particular fields. We shall meet once again next Sunday to see where we stand.

You may go.

Hong Kong, March 2021

Postface

If, after reading this book, you have not learned anything about China, please send your request for your money back to:

david.baverez@lesroismages.fr

New Titles from Westphalia Press

Contests of Initiative: Countering China's Gray Zone Strategy in the East and South China Seas
by Dr. Raymond Kuo

China is engaged in a widespread assertion of sovereignty in the South and East China Seas. It employs a "gray zone" strategy: using coercive but sub-conventional military power to drive off challengers and prevent escalation, while simultaneously seizing territory and asserting maritime control.

Frontline Diplomacy: A Memoir of a Foreign Service Officer in the Middle East
by William A. Rugh

In short vignettes, this book describes how American diplomats working in the Middle East dealt with a variety of challenges over the last decades of the 20th century. Each of the vignettes concludes with an insight about diplomatic practice derived from the experience.

Anti-Poverty Measures in America: Scientism and Other Obstacles
Editors, Max J. Skidmore and Biko Koenig

Anti-Poverty Measures in America brings together a remarkable collection of essays dealing with the inhibiting effects of scientism, an over-dependence on scientific methodology that is prevalent in the social sciences, and other obstacles to anti-poverty legislation.

Geopolitics of Outer Space: Global Security and Development
by Ilayda Aydin

A desire for increased security and rapid development is driving nation-states to engage in an intensifying competition for the unique assets of space. This book analyses the Chinese-American space discourse from the lenses of international relations theory, history and political psychology to explore these questions.

Bunker Diplomacy: An Arab-American in the U.S. Foreign Service
by Nabeel Khoury

After twenty-five years in the Foreign Service, Dr. Nabeel A. Khoury retired from the U.S. Department of State in 2013 with the rank of Minister Counselor. In his last overseas posting, Khoury served as deputy chief of mission at the U.S. embassy in Yemen (2004-2007).

Managing Challenges for the Flint Water Crisis
Edited by Toyna E. Thornton, Andrew D. Williams, Katherine M. Simon, Jennifer F. Sklarew

This edited volume examines several public management and intergovernmental failures, with particular attention on social, political, and financial impacts. Understanding disaster meaning, even causality, is essential to the problem-solving process.

Growing Inequality: Bridging Complex Systems, Population Health, and Health Disparities
Editors: George A. Kaplan, Ana V. Diez Roux, Carl P. Simon, and Sandro Galea

Why is America's health is poorer than the health of other wealthy countries and why health inequities persist despite our efforts? In this book, researchers report on groundbreaking insights to simulate how these determinants come together to produce levels of population health and disparities and test new solutions.

Issues in Maritime Cyber Security
Edited by Dr. Joe DiRenzo III, Dr. Nicole K. Drumhiller, and Dr. Fred S. Roberts

The complexity of making MTS safe from cyber attack is daunting and the need for all stakeholders in both government (at all levels) and private industry to be involved in cyber security is more significant than ever as the use of the MTS continues to grow.

The Politics of Impeachment
Margaret Tseng, Editor

This volume addresses the increased political nature of impeachment. Offering a wide overview of impeachment on the federal and state level, it includes: the politics of bringing impeachment articles forward, the politicized impeachment proceedings, the political nature of how one conducts oneself during the proceedings and the political fallout afterwards.